D1297279

# BIOGRAPHY

# Biography

## A *Game*

### MAX FRISCH

*Translated from the German by Michael Bullock*

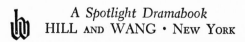

A *Spotlight Dramabook*
HILL AND WANG · NEW YORK

Originally published in German under the title *Biografie: Ein Spiel* by Suhrkamp Verlag, Frankfurt am Main.
Copyright © 1967 by Suhrkamp Verlag

Translation copyright © 1969 by Michael Bullock

Standard book number (clothbound edition): 8090–3034–9
Standard book number (paperback edition): 8090–1217–0

Library of Congress catalog card number: 69–16834

First edition May 1969

All inquiries concerning the rights for professional or amateur stock production should be directed to Joan Daves, 145 East 49th Street, New York, N.Y. 10017

Manufactured in the United States of America by The Colonial Press Inc., Clinton, Massachusetts

I often wonder what it would be like if we were to start our life all over again. Consciously, I mean. If our first life had been, as it were, only a rough copy and our second, a fair one. In that case, I believe, every one of us would first of all do his utmost not to repeat himself. At least he would create a different environment for himself. He would, for instance, get himself a place like this, with flowers and full of light. I have a wife and two little girls. My wife, I'm sorry to say, always complains of being poorly, and so on and so forth. Well, if I had to start my life all over again, I wouldn't get married. . . . No, certainly not.

VERSHININ in Chekhov's The Three Sisters

# BIOGRAPHY

# CHARACTERS

Kürmann
Antoinette
Recorder
Snot (Snottler), *a ten-year-old boy*
The Old Rector
A Corporal
Kürmann's Mother
Nurse
Doctor
Helen, *a mulatto*
Kürmann's Father
The Bride
Kürmann's Mother-in-law
Kürmann's Father-in-law
A Child, *dressed as bridesmaid*
An Evangelical Pastor
Thomas, *Kürmann's son*
A Refugee
His Wife and Two Children
Frau Hubalek
Professor Krolevsky
Ballet Pupils

A Ballet Master
A Waiter
Two Security Policemen
Henrik, *an advertising consultant*
His Wife
Schneider
His Wife
Party Guests
Hornacher, *the new rector*
Pina, *an Italian girl*
Egon Stahel
His Wife
Snottler, *a commercial attaché*
Marlis
Doctor's Assistant
Two Gentlemen in Cap and Gown
Two Undertaker's Men
Members of Funeral Procession
Two Stagehands
Ambulance Men

# AUTHOR'S NOTE

The play takes place on the stage. No attempt should be made to conceal from the audience that they are seeing a locale that is identical with itself: the stage. What is being presented is what can only be shown in a game: the different course events might have taken in someone's life. The subject of the play is not Herr Kürmann's biography, which is banal, but his relationship to the fact that with the passage of time one inevitably acquires a biography. The events are not portrayed illusionistically as taking place in the present, but are reflected upon—as in chess, when we reconstruct the decisive moves of a lost game, curious to find out whether and where the game could have been played differently.

The play does not set out to prove anything.

The Recorder, who is in charge of the game, does not represent any metaphysical authority. He puts into words what Kürmann himself knows, or could know. He is not a *compère*: he never turns to the audience but assists Kürmann by objectifying him. If the Recorder (who, by the way, is never addressed by this or any other title) represents any authority, it is the authority of the theatre, which permits what reality does not permit: to repeat, to try out, to change. Thus he has a certain kindness. The dossier he uses is not a diary that Kürmann once wrote, nor is it the sort of dossier assembled by a civil authority. This dossier, whether written or not, exists in Kürmann's consciousness. It is the sum of everything that has become history, his history, which he does not acknowledge as the only possible one. The alternation of acting light and working light does not represent the alternation of illusion and reality. The acting light indicates that a variation is being tried out, a variation of the reality that never appears on the stage. To this extent the play remains a continual rehearsal. When Kürmann emerges from a scene, he does not do so as an actor but as Kürmann, and it may even be that he then appears more credible. No scene fits him in such a way that it might not also have been different. He alone cannot be different.

I intended the play to be a comedy.

# PART ONE

*When the curtain rises, the working light is on. The whole stage is visible. In the center stands the furniture, representing a modern living-room when the stage is lit for acting: a desk on the right, on the left a sofa, an easy chair, and a floor lamp; a bookcase is suspended in mid-air; no other walls.*

*A young lady in an evening dress is sitting in the easy chair, waiting; she is wearing horn-rimmed spectacles. Silence. Then a cracked piano is heard from the next room—bars broken off in the middle, repetition as though the player is practicing, then silence again. The young lady goes on waiting. Finally a gentleman enters with a dossier and goes to a lectern in the left foreground that does not form part of the room. He places the dossier on the lectern and switches on a neon lamp.*

RECORDER. Right. He has just said, if he could start his life all over again, he knows exactly what he would do differently. [*The young lady smiles.*] You don't mind if we let him make fresh choices? [*The young lady nods.*] For example, he would like to repeat his first meeting with you. [*He leafs through the dossier, then reads out.*] "May 26, 1960. I had guests. It got late. When the guests had finally left, she was just sitting there. What can you do with an unknown woman who doesn't leave, who just sits there without speaking at two in the morning? It need not have happened." [*He switches off the neon lamp.*] Go ahead.

*Acting light. Voices outside, laughter, finally silence; soon afterward* KÜRMANN *enters whistling to himself until he sees the young lady.*

ANTOINETTE. I'm going soon too.

*Silence; he stands there at a loss, then begins to clear away bottles and glasses and ash trays; then he is once more at a loss.*

KÜRMANN. Don't you feel well?

ANTOINETTE. On the contrary. [*She takes a cigarette.*] Just one more cigarette. [*She waits in vain for a light.*[ If I'm not in the way. [*She lights her cigarette and smokes.*] I enjoyed it very much. Some of them were very nice, I thought, very stimulating. . . . [*Silence.*] Have you anything left to drink?

5

KÜRMANN *goes to a small liquor cabinet and pours out a whisky; he makes a business of it to emphasize his silence, polite in the manner of a host left with no alternative.*

KÜRMANN. Ice? [*He hands her the whisky.*]

ANTOINETTE. What about you?

KÜRMANN. I have to work tomorrow.

ANTOINETTE. What do you do?

*A clock strikes two.*

KÜRMANN. It's two o'clock.

ANTOINETTE. Are you expecting someone?

KÜRMANN. On the contrary.

ANTOINETTE. You're tired.

KÜRMANN. I'm ready to drop.

ANTOINETTE. Why don't you sit down? [KÜRMANN *remains standing and says nothing.*] I can't drink any quicker. [*Silence.*] I really only wanted to hear your old musical clock again. Musical clocks fascinate me. The way the figures always go through the same movements as soon as the music starts. It always plays the same waltz, and yet you can't wait to see what happens each time. Don't you feel the same? [*She slowly empties her glass.*]

KÜRMANN. Another whisky?

*She stubs out her cigarette.*

ANTOINETTE. I'm going now.

KÜRMANN. Have you a car?

ANTOINETTE. No.

KÜRMANN. May I give you a lift?

ANTOINETTE. I thought you were tired.

KÜRMANN. Not in the least.

ANTOINETTE. Nor am I. [*She takes another cigarette.*] Why are you looking at me like that? Have you a light? Why are you looking at me like that?

KÜRMANN *gives her a light, then goes to the liquor cabinet and pours himself a whisky; he stands with his back to her, his glass in his hand, without drinking.*

KÜRMANN. Did you say something?

ANTOINETTE. No.

KÜRMANN. Nor did I. [*Silence; she smokes nonchalantly;* KÜRMANN *looks at her; then he sits down in an armchair, crosses his legs, and shows that he is waiting. Silence.*] What do you think of Wittgenstein?

ANTOINETTE. Wittgenstein? Why Wittgenstein?

KÜRMANN. For example. [*He drinks.*] We can't just sit here saying nothing until dawn breaks and the birds begin to twitter. [*He drinks.*] What do you think of the Krolevsky case?

ANTOINETTE. Who is Krolevsky?

KÜRMANN. Professor Krolevsky. He was here this evening. Professor Vladimir Krolevsky. What do you think of Marxism-Leninism? Or I could ask, how old are you?

ANTOINETTE. Twenty-nine.

KÜRMANN. What do you do? Where do you live?

ANTOINETTE. In Paris at the moment.

KÜRMANN. You know, quite frankly it doesn't really interest me, not in the least. I'm simply asking for the sake of something to say, in order to be polite. At two in the morning. You're forcing me to display a curiosity I don't really feel. Quite frankly. And, you know, I only said that so someone should be speaking in this room at two in the morning. [*He drinks.*] That's all too familiar!

ANTOINETTE. What is?

KÜRMANN. The more silent the lady, the more convinced the man is that he is responsible for their boredom. And the more I drink, the less I can think of to say, and the less I can think of to say, the more frankly, the more personally I shall talk, simply because there are only the two of us. At two in the morning. [*He drinks.*] That's all too familiar! And yet you're not listening to me at all, believe me, not at all. You sit there smoking and not saying anything, just waiting until nothing else occurs to me except what you might call the naked fact that we are a man and a woman——

*She stubs out her cigarette.*

ANTOINETTE. Why don't you ring for a taxi?

KÜRMANN. As soon as you ask me to.

*Pause.*

ANTOINETTE. I really am listening to you.

KÜRMANN *stands up.*

KÜRMANN. Do you play chess?

ANTOINETTE. No.

KÜRMANN. Then you can learn tonight.

ANTOINETTE. Why? [KÜRMANN *goes out.*] Why don't you ring for a taxi?

KÜRMANN *comes back with a chess set.*

KÜRMANN. Look. These are the pawns. They can't move backwards. This is a knight. And then there are the rooks. Look, these are bishops. One on white, one on black. This is the queen. She can do anything. The king. [*Pause, until he has set up all the pieces.*] I'm not tired, but we won't speak until dawn starts to break and the birds are twittering outside, not a word. [*She picks up her handbag and rises.*] You can sleep here, but it would be better if you didn't. To be frank, I'd rather you didn't. [*She sits down on the sofa to apply lipstick;* KÜRMANN *sits in front of the chessboard and fills his pipe, his eyes on the board.*] It's your move.

ANTOINETTE. I have to work tomorrow as well.

KÜRMANN. You're white, because you're the guest. [*He lights his pipe.*] I'm not drunk, and neither are you; we both know what we don't want. [*He strikes a second match.*] I'm not in love. [*He strikes a third match.*] You see, I'm already talking very confidentially, and that's just what I didn't want, and I don't even know your name.

ANTOINETTE. Antoinette.

KÜRMANN. We've only just met for the first time. I hope you won't mind if I don't call you by your Christian name.

ANTOINETTE. Stein.

KÜRMANN. Fräulein Stein——

*She closes her tube of lipstick.*

ANTOINETTE. I don't play chess. [*She takes her powder compact.*]

KÜRMANN. I'll explain the moves as we go along. You start with the king's pawn. Good. I cover—also with the king's pawn. Now you bring out your knight. [*She powders her face.*] Fräulein Stein, I have a high regard for you.

ANTOINETTE. Why?

KÜRMANN. I don't know, but if we don't play chess now, I know what will happen: I shall adore you in a way that will amaze everyone, I shall spoil you. I'm good at that. I shall wait on you hand and foot; you're just the sort for that. I shall imagine I can't live without Antoinette Stein. I shall make a destiny of it. For seven years. I shall wait on you hand and foot until we need two lawyers. [*She snaps her powder compact shut.*] Let's play chess. [*She rises.*] What are you looking for?

ANTOINETTE. My jacket.

*KÜRMANN rises and gives her the jacket.*

KÜRMANN. We shall be grateful to one another, Antoinette, for seven years, if you now let me ring for a taxi.

ANTOINETTE. Please do.

*KÜRMANN goes to the telephone and rings for a taxi.*

KÜRMANN. He's coming right away.

ANTOINETTE. Thank you.

KÜRMANN. I thank you. [*Pause. They look at each other.*] Like two cats. Miaow. You must hiss. Sss. Otherwise I'll hiss. Sss. [*She rises and takes a cigarette.*] Miaow, miaow, miaow. [*She lights the cigarette.*] You do it wonderfully, the way you almost close your eyes when you're smoking, the way they narrow to slits, like they are now—wonderful.

ANTOINETTE. Sss.

KÜRMANN. Miaow.

ANTOINETTE. Miaow.

BOTH. Miaow-iaow-iaow. [*They laugh.*]

ANTOINETTE. Joking apart.

KÜRMANN. Joking apart. [*He takes off her jacket.*]

ANTOINETTE. What are you doing? [*The doorbell rings.*] There's my taxi.

KÜRMANN. Joking apart. [*He takes off her horn-rimmed spectacles.*]

ANTOINETTE. At least put the light out.

KÜRMANN. Can we start again?

*Neon lamp on.*

RECORDER. Where do you want to start from?

KÜRMANN. The moment when the clock strikes two.

RECORDER. As you like.

KÜRMANN *gives back the horn-rimmed spectacles.*

KÜRMANN. Sorry.

ANTOINETTE. That's all right. [*She sits down in the easy chair.*]

*The neon lamp goes out.*

RECORDER. Go ahead.

*A clock strikes two.*

ANTOINETTE. "I really only wanted to hear your old musical clock again. Musical clocks fascinate me. The way the figures always go through the same movements as soon as the music starts. It always plays the same waltz, and yet you can't wait to see what happens each time."

KÜRMANN. I know.

ANTOINETTE. "Don't you feel the same?"

KÜRMANN *goes to the musical clock and winds it up; there is a gay tinkling; he goes on winding until the waltz is over.*

KÜRMANN. Is there anything else I can do for you? [*He goes to the liquor cabinet.*] I'm afraid there's no whisky left.

ANTOINETTE. It doesn't matter. [*She takes a cigarette.*] What do you think of Wittgenstein?

KÜRMANN *pours himself a whisky.*

KÜRMANN. "I have to work tomorrow."

ANTOINETTE. "What do you do?"

KÜRMANN *drinks.*

RECORDER. Why don't you tell her?

ANTOINETTE. "What do you do?"

KÜRMANN. Behavior studies. [*He drinks.*]

RECORDER. Go on!

KÜRMANN. Frau Hubalek comes at eight.

ANTOINETTE. Who is Frau Hubalek?

KÜRMANN. My housekeeper.

RECORDER. Stop!

*Neon lamp on.*

RECORDER. You can't say that, Herr Kürmann. You no sooner see a young lady in your flat at two in the morning than you're already thinking that your housekeeper comes at eight.

KÜRMANN. Let's start again.

RECORDER. And then you say there's no whisky left, and you've no sooner lied than you take another bottle and pour yourself a whisky.

ANTOINETTE. I didn't even notice that.

KÜRMANN. Let's start again!

RECORDER. From the beginning?

KÜRMANN. Please.

RECORDER. As you like.

KÜRMANN. Why is she suddenly not wearing glasses?

RECORDER. That's up to the lady. You can't tell her what to do, Herr Kürmann. What you can choose is your own behavior. Don't worry about whether she's wearing horn-rimmed spectacles or not. And don't keep thinking: that's all too familiar. You come in, whistling to yourself, a man at the pinnacle of his career. You've just been made a professor——

KÜRMANN. I know.

RECORDER. They've just had a surprise party in your honor; you see your wife for the first time. Completely relaxed.

KÜRMANN. That's easily said.

RECORDER. Completely relaxed.

*KÜRMANN goes out.*

ANTOINETTE. From the beginning?

RECORDER. If you don't mind.

*Neon lamp off.*

ANTOINETTE. Shall I wear the glasses or not?

*Voices outside, laughter, then silence; soon afterward* KÜRMANN *enters whistling to himself until he sees the young lady in the easy chair.*

ANTOINETTE. "I'm going soon too."

KÜRMANN. "Don't you feel well?"

ANTOINETTE. "On the contrary." [*She takes a cigarette.*] "Just one more cigarette." [*She waits in vain for a light and lights the cigarette herself.*] "If I'm not in the way." [*She smokes.*] "I enjoyed it very much. Some of them were very nice, I thought, very stimulating. . . ."

KÜRMANN *says nothing.*

RECORDER. Go on! [KÜRMANN *goes and pours out whisky.*] Don't start thinking about Frau Hubalek.

KÜRMANN *hands a whisky to* ANTOINETTE.

ANTOINETTE. "What about you?"

KÜRMANN. "I have to work tomorrow."

ANTOINETTE. "What do you do?"

*Pause.*

RECORDER. Now you've gone silent again.

ANTOINETTE *puts on her horn-rimmed spectacles.*

ANTOINETTE. "Why are you looking at me like that?"

RECORDER. The longer you say nothing, the more ambiguous the silence becomes. Don't you feel that? The more intimately you will have to talk afterwards.

ANTOINETTE. "Why are you looking at me like that?"

*A clock strikes two.*

KÜRMANN. "It's two o'clock."

ANTOINETTE. "I'm going."

KÜRMANN. "Have you a car?"

ANTOINETTE. Yes. [*She smokes nonchalantly.*]

KÜRMANN. Before she said No, she hadn't a car. Now she says Yes, so that I can't ring for a taxi. I'll never get her out of this flat!

*The* RECORDER *steps into the scene.*

RECORDER. May I tell you the mistake you are making from the very outset? You no sooner see a young woman in this room, a stranger, than you start thinking of a story you've been through before. Right? That's why you're scared, don't know what to say——

KÜRMANN. I want her to go.

RECORDER. So that she doesn't become your wife.

KÜRMANN. Yes.

RECORDER. You see, your behavior isn't governed by the present, but by a memory. That's the trouble. You think you already know the future because of your past experience. That's why it turns out to be the same story every time.

KÜRMANN. Why doesn't she go?

RECORDER. She can't.

KÜRMANN. Why not?

RECORDER. If she now takes her handbag and stands up, it means she has guessed what you are thinking, and that would be embarrassing for you. Why don't you talk about behavior studies? In a way anyone can understand. Why do you assume that the young lady wants what you don't want? The ambiguity comes from you.

KÜRMANN. H'm.

RECORDER. You think you know women because every time you meet a woman you repeat the same mistake.

KÜRMANN. Go on!

RECORDER. It's your fault if she doesn't go. [*The* RECORDER *returns to his desk.*] All right.

*A clock strikes two.*

KÜRMANN. "It's two o'clock."

*She stubs out her cigarette.*

ANTOINETTE. "Are you expecting someone?"

KÜRMANN. Yes.

RECORDER. Good.

KÜRMANN. But not a woman.

RECORDER. Very good.

KÜRMANN. I'm expecting a boy. [*She takes her handbag.*] I'm expecting a boy.

RECORDER. But don't say it twice, as though you didn't believe it yourself. And don't say a boy. Only the uninitiated talk like that. Say a student who plays chess. A highly gifted young man. A child prodigy whom you are helping. Talk about his genius. That will do the trick.

KÜRMANN. Was that a knock?

ANTOINETTE. I didn't hear anything.

KÜRMANN. I hope nothing has happened to him.

RECORDER. Good.

KÜRMANN. I get so scared every night——

*She crumples up the cigarette pack.*

ANTOINETTE. Now I haven't got a single cigarette left!

KÜRMANN *lights his pipe.*

KÜRMANN. A student . . . highly gifted. . . . Unfortunately he is pathologically jealous. If he comes along and finds a woman in my flat at two in the morning, he's quite capable of shooting.

RECORDER. Don't exaggerate.

KÜRMANN. A Sicilian . . . but blond, you know, blond with blue eyes. . . . That comes from the Normans. . . . On the other hand, his mouth is Greek. . . . He's a musical prodigy. . . . And he's a great-grandson of Pirandello.

RECORDER. Now you're talking too much.

ANTOINETTE. I hope nothing has happened to him. [KÜRMANN *smokes his pipe hurriedly.*] Wouldn't you like to ring up?

KÜRMANN. Where!

ANTOINETTE. Have you a cigarette left?

KÜRMANN. Take my pipe. [*He wipes the mouthpiece and gives her the pipe.*]

ANTOINETTE. What about you?

KÜRMANN. It's a light tobacco, EARLY MORNING PIPE. [*She puts the pipe in her mouth.*] You must keep what I've just told you to yourself, Fräulein Stein. The University knows nothing about it. [*She coughs.*] You have to suck, slowly and regularly. [*He takes the pipe and shows her how to smoke.*] You see? Like that. [*He wipes the pipe and hands it back to her.*] Slowly and regularly.

*She smokes slowly and regularly.*

ANTOINETTE. Can you think at the same time?

KÜRMANN. It mustn't get hot.

*She smokes slowly and regularly.*

ANTOINETTE. All my friends, I mean all my real friends, live like you. [*She puffs out smoke.*] Almost all of them. [*She puffs out smoke.*] The other men are terrible, you know. They almost always misunderstand a woman sooner or later.

KÜRMANN. Is that so?

ANTOINETTE. Yes. [*She coughs.*]

KÜRMANN. Slowly and regularly.

*She smokes slowly and regularly.*

ANTOINETTE. If it wasn't for Claude-Philippe!

KÜRMANN. Who is Claude-Philippe?

ANTOINETTE. My friend in Paris. I live with him. A real friend. I can do just as I like. I can come and go, and he always understands.

KÜRMANN. What else does he do?

ANTOINETTE. He's a dancer.

KÜRMANN. Ah.

ANTOINETTE. All other men, almost all, are a bore, even intelligent men. No sooner are there just the two of you than they get confidential or nervous, and suddenly all they can think of is that I'm a young woman. Hardly any of them ever ask what I do for a living, and if I talk about my work, they look at my lips. It's terrible. No sooner are you alone with them in a flat at two in the morning than they start thinking heaven knows what—you can't imagine what it's like! And at the same time they're frightened of it, especially the intellectuals. [*She sucks at the pipe.*] Now it's gone out. [KÜRMANN *takes the pipe to relight it.*] I'm glad I've met you, very glad.

KÜRMANN. Why?

ANTOINETTE. I haven't any brothers. [*She stands up.*]

KÜRMANN. Are you going already?

ANTOINETTE. I have to work tomorrow too.

KÜRMANN. What do you do?

ANTOINETTE. I'm a translator. I'm from Alsace. Claude-Philippe is a great help to me; he doesn't know any German, but he has such a feeling for it—incredible. . . . [*Pause.*] I really hope nothing has happened to him.

KÜRMANN *helps her into the jacket of her evening dress.*

Kürmann. If I can ever help you in any way——

Antoinette. You're very sweet.

Kürmann *takes her hands.*

Recorder. Stop! [*Switches on neon lamp.*] Why do you take hold of her hands now? Instead of standing there like a brother, with your hands in your pockets, such feelings and so on, but with your hands in your pockets like a brother with his sister. [Kürmann *tries it.*] But relaxed! [*The* Recorder *steps into the scene, takes off the jacket again, and takes* Kürmann's *place to show him how to do it.*] What was your last line?

Antoinette. "I haven't any brothers."

Recorder. And what do you say then?

Kürmann. That wasn't her last line.

Antoinette. "All my friends, I mean my real friends who are friends for life, are homosexuals. Almost all of them. All of them really."

Recorder. And what do you say then?

Kürmann. That's not right.

Antoinette. "If it wasn't for Claude-Philippe."

Kürmann. I believe that, but she said that earlier, that she had a real friend in Paris, a dancer. I can't reply to that by saying, "If I can ever help you in any way."

Recorder. What was his last line?

Kürmann. "If I can ever help you in any way."

Recorder. What do you say now?

Antoinette. "You're very sweet."

*The* Recorder *gives her the jacket.*

Kürmann. I'm sorry, but that's not right. If I don't give her the jacket till now, how am I to have my hands in my pockets when she starts getting affectionate? You just try it.

*The* Recorder *takes back the jacket.*

Recorder. Right, go on.

Antoinette. "I'm glad I've met you, very glad."

Recorder. Go on.

Antoinette. "I haven't any brothers."

Recorder. We've heard that.

KÜRMANN. "What do you do?"

ANTOINETTE. "I'm a translator."

RECORDER. No——

ANTOINETTE. "I'm from Alsace."

RECORDER. ——your last line before the jacket!

KÜRMANN. "Claude-Philippe doesn't know any German, but he has such a feeling for it."

ANTOINETTE. "Incredible."

RECORDER. What do you say then?

KÜRMANN. Nothing. I wonder how Frenchmen who don't know German can have a feeling for it. Pause! I admit I could have asked now: what are you translating?

ANTOINETTE. Adorno.

RECORDER. But you didn't say that.

ANTOINETTE. Because he didn't ask.

KÜRMANN. Because I want her to go. I ask myself: why doesn't she stay in Paris? But that's none of my business. Pause. And because I pause, she imagines I'm now thinking of my boy.

ANTOINETTE. "I really hope nothing has happened to him."

RECORDER. Go on!

KÜRMANN. "Are you going already?"

ANTOINETTE. "I have to work tomorrow too."

KÜRMANN. "What do you do?"

ANTOINETTE. "I'm a translator."

RECORDER. Not again!

ANTOINETTE. "I'm from Alsace."

*The* RECORDER *lets the jacket sink.*

RECORDER. Please let's have the last line before Kürmann gives you your jacket and makes the mistake of taking hold of your hands.

KÜRMANN. Why is that a mistake?

RECORDER. The pressure of your hands will give you away.

ANTOINETTE. "The other men are terrible, you know. They almost always misunderstand a woman sooner or later."

KÜRMANN. "Is that so?"

ANTOINETTE. "Yes."

*The* Recorder *gives her the jacket.*

Recorder. "If I can ever help you in any way——"

Antoinette. "You're very sweet."

*The* Recorder *puts his hands in his pockets; then he steps back out of the part.*

Recorder. Got it? Like a brother with his sister. Even if you now give her a kiss, which is possible, don't forget that you're expecting a young Sicilian. Otherwise she wouldn't kiss you. She is relieved that you aren't an ordinary man, Herr Kürmann, not even when you're alone together.

Kürmann. I get it.

Recorder. Give her the jacket again. [Kürmann *takes back the jacket.*] Right.

*She takes a cigarette.*

Antoinette. So there were some cigarettes left. [Kürmann *gives her a light.*] Why didn't I stay in Paris? I should like to start a small publishing firm, my own firm, where I can do what I like. That's why I'm here. And if nothing comes of the publishing firm, I shall do something else. [*She smokes.*] Something on my own. [*She smokes.*] Best of all, I should like to run a little gallery——

Recorder. You hear that?

Kürmann. Why didn't she say anything about that?

Recorder. She wants a life of her own; she isn't looking for a man who thinks she can't live without him and who buys a revolver when he sees one day that she can live without him.

Antoinette. If you want to know, a very much younger man, younger than Kürmann, drove me here, an architect, who wants to go to Brazil with me. [*She laughs.*] What could I do in Brazil? [*She smokes.*] That's why I stayed so long—because I was afraid he was waiting for me downstairs.

Kürmann. How was I to know that?

Antoinette. That's why I wanted a taxi, in case he was standing by my car waiting. [*She smokes.*] I don't want any fuss. [*She stubs out her cigarette.*] Can I have my jacket now?

Kürmann *stands motionless.*

Recorder. What are you thinking about?

Kürmann. Adorno.

RECORDER. It's too late now. You know now what you could have talked to the young lady about: about Hegel, about Schönberg, about Kierkegaard, about Beckett——

ANTOINETTE. I did my doctorate with Adorno.

RECORDER. Why don't you give her the jacket?

KÜRMANN *gives her the jacket.*

KÜRMANN. "If I can ever help you in any way——"

ANTOINETTE. "You're very sweet."

KÜRMANN *puts his hands in his pockets.*

KÜRMANN. What kind of car have you got?

RECORDER. Good.

KÜRMANN. Don't forget your handbag.

RECORDER. If you don't make any more mistakes now, in the elevator, you'll have done it: a biography without Antoinette.

KÜRMANN *switches off the ceiling light.*

KÜRMANN. I'll take you to the car. [*She sits down.*] Why is she suddenly so pale?

RECORDER. That's from the pipe.

*She lies in the easy chair, eyes closed; her handbag has fallen on the floor.*

KÜRMANN. I don't believe her.

*The* RECORDER *steps into the scene to feel her pulse, while* KÜRMANN *stands to one side filling his pipe.*

RECORDER. It's really a minor collapse. You and your EARLY MORNING PIPE! Don't keep saying, it's all too familiar. Her forehead is as cold as ice. [KÜRMANN *lights his pipe.*] Do you have to smoke now? Instead of opening a window. You're behaving impossibly, like a brute.

KÜRMANN. Better now than in seven years.

RECORDER. As you like. [*She rises.*] She can't possibly drive.

ANTOINETTE. I must get home. . . .

RECORDER. Can't you see that?

ANTOINETTE. I must lie down. . . .

RECORDER. You're risking a life. [*She takes off the jacket of her evening dress.*] Aren't you going to fetch a glass of cold water?

The least you can do when a guest is dizzy is to fetch a glass of cold water.

KÜRMANN *goes out.*

ANTOINETTE. I'm sorry . . . [*She undoes her evening dress; she has to lie down in order not to faint. When* KÜRMANN *comes back with the glass of water, she is lying on the sofa.*] I'm sorry . . .

KÜRMANN. Drink this.

ANTOINETTE. That has never happened to me before—suddenly—to feel so giddy. . . .

KÜRMANN. Shall I fetch a doctor?

ANTOINETTE. Don't look at me. [*Pause.*] I feel ashamed.

RECORDER. You'll catch cold.

KÜRMANN. It's all too familiar——

RECORDER. Won't you fetch a rug?

KÜRMANN. ——I fetch a rug, then I take my handkerchief and wipe her forehead, her temples, her forehead, her eyelids. I know how I act the Good Samaritan. I shall make coffee, watch over her, in silence, watch over her, take off her shoes so she feels more comfortable, and in the end she'll say, at least put the light out! [*Pause.*] It's nothing to be ashamed of, Antoinette; it could have happened to anyone, Antoinette; it's nothing to be ashamed of. [*He takes off her shoes.*]

ANTOINETTE. What are you doing?

KÜRMANN. You'll feel more comfortable like that. [*He puts the shoes down on the carpet.*]

ANTOINETTE. At least put the light out.

*Blackout.*

KÜRMANN. Stop! Who put the light out? Stop!

*Working light. The whole stage is visible again.*

RECORDER. Don't you want to go on?

KÜRMANN. No.

RECORDER. As you like.

ANTOINETTE *tidies her evening dress.*

ANTOINETTE. Where are my shoes?

KÜRMANN. I beg your pardon?

ANTOINETTE. Where are my shoes?

KÜRMANN *gives her the shoes.*

RECORDER. You said, if you could begin your life all over again, you knew exactly what you would do differently——

KÜRMANN. That's right.

RECORDER. Then why do you always do the same thing?

ANTOINETTE *puts on her shoes.*

ANTOINETTE. He's absolutely right. It didn't have to happen. I wasn't in love either. Not in the least. Not next morning either. [*She has put on her shoes and stands up.*] What came of it—I too would be glad if it hadn't had to happen. . . .

The RECORDER *leafs through the dossier.*

RECORDER. Where would you like to start again?

KÜRMANN. Earlier.

RECORDER. How much earlier?

KÜRMANN. Before that night. Before I became a professor. Before these people came to have a party in my honor. Before I saw Antoinette for the first time.

RECORDER. All right.

ANTOINETTE *takes the jacket of her evening dress.*

ANTOINETTE. Good luck. [*She leaves.*]

KÜRMANN. An idiotic story.

RECORDER. Choose another one.

KÜRMANN. A superfluous story.

RECORDER. You have permission, Herr Professor Kürmann, to start again wherever you like, to choose afresh—— [KÜRMANN *takes a bottle of whisky.*] Do you hear? [KÜRMANN *pours whisky.*] You drink too much.

KÜRMANN. What business is that of yours?

RECORDER. I'm only putting into words what you know yourself.

KÜRMANN *stands, drinking.*

KÜRMANN. Who are you actually?

RECORDER. I? [*Turning the pages.*] This here is the life you've led up to now. Till your middle forties. A life that bears looking at. A bit ordinary, I admit. But it seems that as a scientist you're quite eminent. The Kürmann reflex—a concept essential to modern behavior studies, I understand. All you need now is an invitation to Princeton.

KÜRMANN. I asked who you are.

RECORDER. I record. [KÜRMANN *does not understand.*] I record what you make of the possibility offered to you here, what you do differently in your life. That's all. What reality does not permit, the theatre permits: to change, to begin again, to try out, to try out another biography——

KÜRMANN *looks into his glass.*

KÜRMANN. Biography! I refuse to believe that our biography, mine or any other, couldn't look different. Completely different. I only need to act differently one single time——

RECORDER. Go ahead.

KÜRMANN. Not to mention chance! [*Pause.*] I can't bear the sight of this room.

RECORDER. As you like. [*The furniture disappears; so does the bookcase. The stage is empty.* KÜRMANN *stands with his glass in his hand, not looking at the transformation.*] Go ahead.

KÜRMANN. Just once in my life—when I was seventeen; I was riding a bicycle, I remember it clearly; it was the moment before a storm, but the storm never broke; there were flashes of lightning, dust whirled up to the height of a house; there was a smell of elder bushes and tar—just once I had an insight. For a quarter of an hour. It was a real insight, I know that. But I can't think it over again. I'm too stupid. [*He drains his glass.*] Too stupid. [*He looks at the* RECORDER.] That's the only thing I want if I can begin again: a different intelligence.

RECORDER. Excuse me——

KÜRMANN. That's all!

RECORDER. ——you don't understand the rules of the game. You have permission to choose again, but with the intelligence you have. That is a given fact. You can train it differently. You're free to do that. You can ask it for advice when you have to make decisions, or not. You can use it how you like, to avoid mistakes or to justify mistakes when you have made them. As you wish. You can specialize it so that it draws attention to itself—as an expert intelligence. Or as a political intelligence. Or you can let your intelligence go to wrack and ruin: in a religious faith or in alcohol. Or you can preserve it—by confining yourself to skepticism. As you wish. But you cannot change the scope, or let us say, the basic potential, the atomic structure, of your brain. Do you understand? That is a given fact.

ANTOINETTE *appears in an overcoat.*

KÜRMANN. What does she want this time?

ANTOINETTE. My handbag. [KÜRMANN *refuses to help.*] I left my handbag behind.

KÜRMANN. I said, before I saw my wife for the first time! So she can't have left anything here.

*The* RECORDER *indicates to* ANTOINETTE *with a polite gesture that she is in the way, and* ANTOINETTE *retires into the background.*

RECORDER. Do you want your school days over again?

*Change of lighting. A ten-year-old boy appears, dressed in winter clothes.*

RECORDER. You remember little Snot?

SNOT.          Kürmann, you're a rotten shot.
               What a cheesy face you've got.
               Hee, hee, hee,
               Can't hit me.

KÜRMANN. Shut up.

SNOT.          Cheese face, cheese face,
               Can't hit me.

RECORDER. They used to tease you because you once told them in grammar school that you would one day be a professor. Does it still annoy you? You became a professor thirty-three years later, in 1960. [*Three gentlemen appear in the gown of the university, the* RECTOR *carrying a document, which he unrolls.*] Just a moment, your Magnificence, just a moment.

KÜRMANN. I know the document.

SNOT.          Kürmann, you're a rotten shot.
               What a cheesy face you've got.
               Hee, hee, hee,
               Can't hit me.

RECORDER. You know what happened then.

SNOT.  Cheese face, cheese face,
Can't hit me.

ANTOINETTE. What happened? He never told me about that. What did you do to this little fellow?

SNOT *makes a snowball.*

RECORDER. That would be 1927.

KÜRMANN. Yes.

RECORDER. That would mean——

KÜRMANN. Primary school over again

RECORDER. puberty over again

KÜRMANN. final exams over again

RECORDER. your mother's death over again

KÜRMANN. military service over again!

RECORDER. ——that too.

*Soldiers are heard singing.*

CORPORAL [*offstage*]. Squad, *halt!* Left—*face!* Right—*face!* Order—*arms!* At ease!

KÜRMANN. All that over again?

CORPORAL. Atten—*shun!* [*He appears.*] Sir——

RECORDER. Just a moment, Corporal, just a moment.

CORPORAL. At ease!

SNOT *tries to leave.*

RECORDER. Stay here.

SNOT. But my name isn't Snot.

RECORDER. What is it then?

KÜRMANN. His name is Snottler. We called him Snot because he never had a handkerchief.

RECORDER. Stay here. [*He goes to the boy and leads him back to his place.*] Perhaps you won't lose your left eye. Do you hear? Perhaps you won't lose your left eye.

*The* CORPORAL *clicks his heels.*

CORPORAL. Atten—*shun!*

RECORDER. Corporal——

CORPORAL. Right shoulder—*arms!*

RECORDER. If I may ask you——

CORPORAL. Forward—*march!* [*The sound of marching footsteps.*] Dress by the right! Eyes—*front!* Left, right, left, right! Dress by the left! Eyes—*front!* Left, right, left, right! [*The* CORPORAL *leaves, following the invisible column. After a time his command is heard.*] Left, right, left, right. . . .

*Silence.*

RECTOR. May I read out the document now? It represents, I think I may say, a high point in the life of our esteemed colleague. His appointment as professor and Director of the Institute for Behavior Studies——

KÜRMANN. Stay where you are.

RECORDER. Perhaps Herr Kürmann doesn't want any high points, perhaps Herr Kürmann would like to see his mother again.

*A* NURSE *dressed in white appears. She wheels in a white bed and bends over an old woman who lies in the bed without moving.*

NURSE. Frau Kürmann? I can't hear you. What did you say? I can't understand a word, Frau Kürmann——

*A* DOCTOR *appears with a hypodermic syringe.*

RECORDER. Perhaps all she could have said would have been some trifling thing like, you shouldn't drink, you should marry, you should always wear warm socks.

*A young mulatto appears, wearing a bikini and an open blouse over it. She is barefoot; her feet are wet.*

HELEN. What's the matter?

KÜRMANN. My mother is dying.

HELEN. What are you going to do?

*The* DOCTOR *gives* KÜRMANN'S MOTHER *an injection.*

DOCTOR. She'll sleep. Her heart is very strong. In three hours give her another injection. I shall be at home. [*He leaves.*]

NURSE. Frau Kürmann? [*The* NURSE *leaves.*]

HELEN. Why don't you go to Europe?

KÜRMANN. Helen——

HELEN. Why don't you go?

*A boat appears, of a kind that goes with* HELEN. *She jumps in and takes the oar.*

RECORDER. You didn't want to leave Helen. You were afraid you would lose her if you went off to Europe. Besides, according to the dossier, you had no money just then.

KÜRMANN. Give me the dossier!

RECORDER. Here you are. [*He gives* KÜRMANN *the dossier.*] But there's nothing in it you don't know already. Salary for a year, two hundred dollars a month. After your trip with Helen—you bought an old Ford and hired a boat—you have just eighteen dollars left. Too little even for a sea voyage. You might be able to sell the Ford. Your first car, by the way.

KÜRMANN. I know.

RECORDER. Your father was a master baker.

KÜRMANN. I know.

RECORDER. In debt—he drank. [*A baker appears with a bicycle. He is drunk and beaming with kindliness.*] That would be 1934. It's your seventeenth birthday and your father comes along with a bicycle; it's new and all bright and shiny, the spokes, the handle bars—all shining; it has a head lamp that also shines, a bell, and four gears. An English bicycle. [*The* FATHER *rings the bell.*] Do you remember? [*The* FATHER *rings the bell.*] According to the dossier, it was the fulfillment of your dearest wish. He probably bought it on the installment plan. That was something you never experienced again: the fulfillment of your dearest wish.

KÜRMANN. No.

RECORDER. Would you like the bicycle again?

FATHER. Hannes!

RECORDER. Just a minute, Herr Kürmann, just a minute.

FATHER. Why doesn't he take it?

RECORDER. Just a minute.

*The* FATHER *swears unintelligibly.*

KÜRMANN. ——then I was seventeen.

RECORDER. Exactly.

KÜRMANN. And the snowball fight?

RECORDER. Was over.

KÜRMANN. And he has still lost his eye.

RECORDER. Yes.

*The* NURSE *appears with flowers.*

NURSE. Frau Kürmann, how are you? Better? Look, Frau Kürmann, look. It's a fine day today. I said, it's a fine day outside. Look, Frau Kürmann, look. Flowers from your son in America. [*She unwraps the flowers from their tissue paper.*] Lovely roses.

MOTHER. Hannes——

NURSE. A loving son!

MOTHER. Hannes——

NURSE. So many roses. [*She puts the roses in a vase and leaves.*]

RECORDER. You know how it goes on from there. [*He takes back the dossier and reads.*] "September 1939: Hitler's Germany attacks Poland, declaration of war by Britain and France. You stay in San Francisco. Stalin's Russia also attacks Poland. Spring 1940: Hitler's Germany attacks Holland——"

KÜRMANN. And so on.

RECORDER. "——and Belgium."

KÜRMANN. And so on and so forth.

RECORDER. Why are you losing your nerve? You didn't lose it then. On the contrary, you married. [*A* BRIDE *in white appears.*] Spring 1940: back in Europe to do your military service, you meet your first wife, who later commits suicide. [KÜRMANN *does not look around.*] Would you like to make a different choice here?

BRIDE. Hannes——

RECORDER. Katrin Guggenbühl, twenty-one, blonde with freckles, only child of a pharmacist—you remember? According to the dossier, you knew on the day of the church wedding that the marriage was a mistake. [*Wedding bells.*] Would you like to make a different choice here?

KÜRMANN *catches sight of the* BRIDE. *The* RECORDER *goes over and takes the roses from the vase by the* MOTHER's *bed and puts them in the* BRIDE's *arms.* KÜRMANN *is still holding his empty whisky glass.*

BRIDE. Why don't you speak?

KÜRMANN. Katrin.

BRIDE. What's the matter with you? [KÜRMANN *says nothing.*] Go on, tell me.

*Two* UNDERTAKER'S MEN *bring a coffin and leave again.*

RECORDER. Perhaps Katrin also knows that this marriage is a mistake, and she is just waiting for you to say so. Why don't you say so? She will break down. Maybe. Of course it would be a shock if you said No now, when the bells are already ringing.

BRIDE. Hannes——

RECORDER. Perhaps you might save her life. [*The bells stop ringing.*] Herr Kürmann, we're waiting. [*To the characters.*] Herr Kürmann said, if he could begin his life again, he knew exactly what he would do differently. [*To* KÜRMANN.] The boy is waiting to find out whether he loses his left eye or not. Your mother is waiting; it can only be a matter of hours. The Rector is waiting with the document. Helen, who made you a man, is waiting on the coast north of San Francisco. And the bride is waiting with the roses——

KÜRMANN. ——for me to become guilty of her death.

RECORDER. Or not. [*An organ plays.*] Herr Kürmann, you have the choice all over again.

*A middle-class gentleman with a top hat and a middle-class lady wearing a hat appear. They stand beside the* BRIDE.

FATHER-IN-LAW. Hannes.

KÜRMANN. Father.

MOTHER-IN-LAW. Hannes.

KÜRMANN. Mother.

RECORDER. Are you afraid of your in-laws?

*A* CHILD *appears in bridesmaid's dress and hands the* BRIDE *a posy of daisies.*

CHILD.     Oh, dearest bride, we wish to you
           Happiness and children too.

*The* CHILD *curtsies.*

MOTHER-IN-LAW. Sweet.

*An* EVANGELICAL PASTOR *appears.*

RECORDER. Are you afraid of an Evangelical minister? He can't know that he is blessing a mistake. Why don't you speak? You remember: according to the dossier, you are wearing a hired morning suit whose sleeves are unfortunately too long. Every time you pray, you have to pull the sleeves back before you can fold your hands. Out in front of the altar, according to the dossier, what you are chiefly thinking about are the sleeves of the morning coat, and then of the tails, which are also far too long.

KÜRMANN. If she had at least smiled! But she felt ashamed! She was suffering! That was how it started and that was how it went on: she suffered. . . . [KÜRMANN *turns away, not knowing where to put his glass.*]

RECORDER. Herr Kürmann.

KÜRMANN. I can hear the organ, oh yes, I can hear it.

RECORDER. Katrin loves you.

KÜRMANN. That's what she thinks.

RECORDER. She's happy.

KÜRMANN. And that's enough for her.

RECORDER. What do you mean by that?

KÜRMANN. Nothing. [*The* RECORDER *takes the empty glass from him.*] Thanks. [*He takes his pipe out of his pocket.*] I still dream of you, Katrin, even today, and when I wake up, I always think you know.

RECORDER. What do you dream?

KÜRMANN. That's no one's business.

RECORDER. Why did you marry?

KÜRMANN. To forget Helen.

HELEN. What is he telling you?

KÜRMANN. I misused her to forget Helen, and she misused me to have a child.

RECORDER. Why don't you tell her so? [KÜRMANN *shakes his head.*] So it's to stay like that?

KÜRMANN. Yes.

RECORDER. That's final?

KÜRMANN. That's final.

*The organ stops.*

PASTOR. Amen.

KÜRMANN. If I hadn't married Katrin, it's possible that she wouldn't have committed suicide later.

RECORDER. That's what I mean.

KÜRMANN. And what about our son?

*A young boy appears in jeans.*

THOMAS. Dad.

KÜRMANN. I'm not a good father, I'm not a bad father; at times I forget him; I'm not a father all the time, but I am his father. When he swims too far out to sea, I'm scared and shout. I learned Latin over again in order to help him, and when he thinks, I'm pleased, and when he wants to know what I think, I try to explain myself. [*He takes the pipe out of his mouth.*] He exists, can't you see that, he exists!

RECORDER. I understand.

KÜRMANN. ——her child.

RECORDER. You love him.

KÜRMANN. That's not the point. You can't think a child out of the world once it's there. [*He laughs.*] Thomas, tell me——

THOMAS. Dad.

KÜRMANN. ——does a son love his father? Does a father love his son?

THOMAS. Dad, I need money.

KÜRMANN. You see?

THOMAS. I've dented the car.

KÜRMANN. Again?

THOMAS. But I had the right of way.

KÜRMANN. How much?

THOMAS. About three hundred bucks.

KÜRMANN *reaches for his wallet.*

KÜRMANN. Just a minute, though. That can't be right. Driving license at eighteen, born 1942—then this accident with the car couldn't have happened before 1960 at the earliest; that would mean Antoinette was there again.

RECORDER. Correct.

KÜRMANN. But I don't want that!

*The RECORDER leads THOMAS out again.*

RECORDER. His son must be smaller.

*The DOCTOR comes in with the NURSE*

DOCTOR. Frau Kürmann?

NURSE. She said she didn't want any more injections. [*The* DOCTOR *feels her pulse.*] She said she was lying on a steep mountain; that was why no one could visit her. I gave her another injection at midnight.

*The* DOCTOR *closes the dead woman's eyes.*

DOCTOR. Inform the son.

HELEN. Now it's too late.

DOCTOR. And bring me her personal effects. [*The* DOCTOR *leaves the deathbed and walks past* KÜRMANN. *They meet as though in a corridor.*] Yes, Herr Kürmann . . . her death wasn't particularly difficult, I don't think. Only your mother had a very strong heart. Astonishing for her age.

*They shake hands; the* DOCTOR *goes.*

HELEN. Now it's too late.

KÜRMANN. Yes.

HELEN. Why didn't you go?

KÜRMANN. Yes.

HELEN. Because of me?

KÜRMANN. Yes.

HELEN *takes his arm.*

RECORDER. You want to stay with Helen?

KÜRMANN. Yes.

RECORDER. As you like. [*Neon lamp on.*] So you've made up your mind, Herr Kürmann, to begin again after your mother's death. In 1939 you went to the University of California, where you met a student named Helen. [*He reads from the dossier.*] "An excursion to Fort Ross. We have a boat, Helen is refused admission to a motel, the night in the boat—"

KÜRMANN. Yes.

RECORDER. So you stay in America. [*A husband and wife appear with two children in dirty overcoats, carrying suitcases.*] Who are they?

REFUGEE. The young gentleman was very kind; the young gentleman saved our lives.

RECORDER. Is that true?

REFUGEE. In 1940, in the spring.

RECORDER. Do you remember these people?

KÜRMANN. Yes. [*Without looking at the group.*] It was on the frontier. Midnight. They had been discovered in a freight car. Because the little girl coughed. Now they are standing between the lines. Without papers. Jews. One of the guards wanted to arrest them on the spot. I asked him some question or other. That was all. I kept on asking him until they had vanished behind his back. [*The* RECORDER *searches through his dossier.*] That was soon after I got back from the USA, pure chance that I just happened to be at that station at that moment, pure chance. [*Because the refugee woman starts sobbing.*] You won't go to the camp. Don't be afraid. I'm not going to stay in San Francisco.

HELEN. What's the matter?

REFUGEE. The young gentleman is very kind.

KÜRMANN. It cost me very little, but it's possible that this minute saved their lives.

RECORDER. Quite true. [*He reads from the dossier.*] "4/14/1940. I visited my fiancée and missed the last train, so that I had to spend the night at the station——"

REFUGEE. Spring.

RECORDER. One moment. [*He reads from the dossier.*] ". . . a married couple with two children and an old man." [*He looks at the group of refugees.*] The old man is missing.

KÜRMANN. The guard fired. [*Pause.*] I have to go.

HELEN. Why?

KÜRMANN. I have to.

HELEN. Okay.

KÜRMANN. It's not okay, not at all, but I have to leave you. I really have to.

HELEN. You're a coward.

KÜRMANN. Helen——

HELEN. I always knew you were.

KÜRMANN *looks at her helplessly.*

RECORDER. She thinks you're afraid because she's a mulatto. Explain to her that she's wrong.

*Pause.*

HELEN. Okay.

KÜRMANN. Helen?

HELEN. Good luck. [*She exits.*]

KÜRMANN. You explain to her!

*The refugees take their suitcases.*

REFUGEE. The young gentleman is very kind.

*The refugees leave.*

KÜRMANN. How else could I have chosen? . . .

RECORDER. So that's to stay?

KÜRMANN. Yes.

RECORDER. You don't want to go any further back?

KÜRMANN. No.

*A scream. Little* SNOT, *hit in the eye by a snowball, yells and holds his hand over his left eye and runs away.*

RECORDER. So that stays.

*The dead mother is wheeled off.*

KÜRMANN. Yes. . . .

*The boat disappears.*

FATHER. What about me?

KÜRMANN. I can't change the fact that you're a drunkard, a kindly drunkard, an affectionate drunkard, but I can't prevent you from falling downstairs that night or some other night. They found you in the morning in the bakeshop—you, but no bread.

FATHER. What did he say?

KÜRMANN. Thanks for the bike. [*The* FATHER *staggers away.*] Father!

*The bicycle remains.*

CORPORAL [*offstage*]. Squad—*halt!*

RECORDER. Corporal—— [*The* CORPORAL *appears, dripping wet.*] What have you been doing?

CORPORAL. Punishment-swimming.

RECORDER. First Lieutenant Kürmann has just skipped the age of his military service. He doesn't want to repeat those two years in uniform.

KÜRMANN. Three years.

RECORDER. Corporal, we don't need you.

CORPORAL. Very good. Squad, atten—*shun!*

RECORDER. All right, Corporal.

CORPORAL. Squad, double time—*march!* Dress by the left! Dress by the right! Left, right, left, right!

RECORDER. That will do.

KÜRMANN. That's easy to say.

CORPORAL. Squad—*sing!*

A *marching song is heard; the* CORPORAL *follows the invisible column; the song slowly dies away; silence.*

RECORDER. Would you like to hear the document now?

*The* RECTOR *unrolls the document.*

KÜRMANN. Is Katrin still there?

RECORDER. Yes.

KÜRMANN. You go away too.

RECORDER. Do you really want that? [*He reads from the dossier.*] "This morning in the course of an argument with Katrin, who always wants to forgive, I said: Then go and hang yourself. When I came home from the Institute in the afternoon, she had done it. Now she is lying here in the coffin. My guilt is unbearable. 6/11/1949." [KÜRMANN *says nothing.*] She is twenty-nine.

KÜRMANN *looks at her.*

KÜRMANN. You go away too.

BRIDE. Hannes——

KÜRMANN. I have gotten used to my guilt.

*The* BRIDE *steps back; the* PARENTS-IN-LAW *and the* PASTOR, *and a few others who join them, form the funeral procession. The coffin is carried by two* UNDERTAKER'S MEN.

RECORDER. Would you like to see her face again?

KÜRMANN. I haven't forgotten it.

*The funeral procession leaves.*

RECTOR. I understand our colleague completely. The discovery of the Kürmann reflex, a discovery absolutely essential to modern behavior studies, was due to a coincidence. Even if we were to repeat the series of experiments extending over years, who can guarantee that this illuminating coincidence would occur again? I think it would be almost irresponsible for a scientist——

RECORDER. When did this coincidence take place?

KÜRMANN. February '59.

*The RECORDER leafs through the dossier.*

RECTOR. It in no way diminishes your achievement, Professor, if I speak here of coincidence. We know it is not chance that discovers, but the human mind that recognizes the meaning of the chance.

RECORDER. "Sea gull No. 411, experimental series C."

KÜRMANN. Yes.

RECORDER. You don't want to forgo that?

ANTOINETTE. He owes his career to that sea gull.

KÜRMANN. I should like to ask the young lady—for the last time—to grasp the fact that she can't possibly have left anything here.

ANTOINETTE. My handbag.

KÜRMANN. I'm asking for autumn 1959.

RECORDER. Fraülein Stein——

KÜRMANN. Where was she in autumn 1959?

ANTOINETTE. In Paris.

RECORDER. Herr Kürmann wants autumn 1959.

*Antoinette leaves.*

KÜRMANN. Let someone else worry about her handbag.

*The RECTOR rolls up the document.*

RECTOR. Let me know when it's time for me to read out the document.

*The three gentlemen in gowns leave.*

RECORDER. Well then——

*ANTOINETTE comes back again.*

ANTOINETTE. Then please tell my husband to see a doctor. Today. The sooner the better. Before it's too late.

RECORDER. Don't you feel well, Herr Kürmann?

KÜRMANN. Rubbish.

Antoinette. When they know what it is, and when it's too late, they always say: a few years ago it would have been curable, quite a minor matter.

Kürmann. I'll go to the doctor.

Antoinette. Please see that he does.

*The* Recorder *bows and* Antoinette *leaves.*

Recorder. And apart from that, what else would you like to do differently in autumn 1959?

Kürmann. I'm just thinking it over.

*A* Stagehand *wheels the bicycle away.*

Recorder. You remember autumn 1959. [*He leafs through the dossier.*] "Tension between Cuba and the USA. / Nigeria becomes independent. / Eisenhower receives Khrushchev. / Somalia becomes independent. / Soviet moon rocket Lunik II, 160 pounds, crash-lands on the moon."

Kürmann *polishes his glasses.*

Kürmann. Give me the discussion with Krolevsky again. Professor Vladimir Krolevsky, who was later dismissed from his teaching post. That was in December, I think. Our conversation in my flat.

Recorder. Very well.

*Working light. The room is set up again. The cracked piano next door is heard again, always the same bars broken off in the middle and repeated. Since this reconstruction of the set produces a pause, the* Recorder *takes a cigarette. Finally the bookcase is lowered. The* Recorder *stubs out his cigarette. Silence.*

Recorder. Herr Kürmann, here's your flat again.

*Neon lamp off.*

*Acting light.*

Kürmann. What's this thing doing here?

Recorder. Your old musical clock.

Kürmann. Get rid of it!

Recorder. As you like. [*A* Stagehand *removes the musical clock.*] Do you want any other changes? You've only got to say the word. Perhaps you would like the desk on the other side?

KÜRMANN. As though that mattered.

RECORDER. You can choose.

*Again the cracked piano from next door.*

KÜRMANN. Do I have to put up with that?

RECORDER. That's the ballet school. Autumn 1959. You remember, there's a ballet school next door. Unfortunately they always leave the window open.

*Repetition of the same bars, accompanied by the* BALLET MASTER'S *voice; then silence.*

KÜRMANN. Did that go on every day?

RECORDER. Apart from Sundays and bank holidays.

KÜRMANN. No one could stick that.

RECORDER. You stuck it.

KÜRMANN. You say I can choose. . . .

RECORDER. But so can the others. You're not alone in the world, Herr Kürmann, and they have rented the house next door, 18 Klettenhof, in order to open their ballet school. These are given facts. If you can't stand it, why don't you choose another flat?

KÜRMANN. What shall I find there?

RECORDER. We shall see.

KÜRMANN. A power saw, perhaps.

RECORDER. Possibly.

KÜRMANN. Or the railway. Or bells chiming. Or the runway of an airport——

*An ominous sound is heard.*

RECORDER. That was the power saw.

KÜRMANN. Stop.

RECORDER. As you like.

*Another sound is heard.*

KÜRMANN. What's that?

RECORDER. This is a very beautiful district, but they're building. Because it's a very beautiful district. Construction machinery. But that will only last for a year and a half.

KÜRMANN. And what will happen then?

A *third noise is heard.*

RECORDER. A kindergarten. [KÜRMANN *shakes his head.*] You can choose. [*Again the cracked piano next door, the same bars of music broken off, accompanied by the* BALLET MASTER'S *voice; repetition; then silence.*] So you're going to stay in this flat.

KÜRMANN *looks around.*

KÜRMANN. So this is what it was like?

RECORDER. You're surprised at your taste?

FRAU HUBALEK *comes in.*

FRAU HUBALEK. Herr Professor Krolevsky.

KÜRMANN. Show him in.

FRAU HUBALEK *goes and* KROLEVSKY *comes in, a bald-headed man with alert eyes behind rimless spectacles, pale; one imagines incorrectly that he is always smiling. He is wearing a worn overcoat, which he does not take off, and carrying a thin leather briefcase; he holds his hat in his hand. His demeanor is extremely shy. He is short, yet he has a certain air of authority.*

KÜRMANN. I think you sat here. [KROLEVSKY *sits down.*] I suppose you find this funny, Professor Krolevsky. We've had this conversation once before. You know my reasons for not joining any party, my fundamental doubts. I don't need to repeat myself.

KROLEVSKY. No.

KÜRMANN. Will you have a drink?

KROLEVSKY. I never drink.

KÜRMANN *pours himself a whisky.*

KÜRMANN. In short, Professor, I've thought it over. . . . [*Pause.* KÜRMANN *stands drinking.*]

KROLEVSKY. What have you thought over?

KÜRMANN. Our discussion in this room, our private discussion. You there, I here. You need not repeat yourself either, Krolevsky; I know it all. In your eyes I am what is nowadays called a nonconformist, an intellectual who sees through the ruling class, pretty accurately, in any case with horror or at least with disgust; but he leaves it at that. Every now and then I sign an appeal, a declaration for or against—protests for the benefit of my conscience so long as consciences are allowed. Apart from that, the nonconformist works on his career.

KROLEVSKY. Did I say that?

KÜRMANN. You said it differently.

KROLEVSKY. What did I say?

KÜRMANN. You said that work in the Party was the only way to change the world [FRAU HUBALEK *comes in.*] and in the process, of course, the end has to justify the means. Everyone knows that, and that's precisely why I don't join any party. [*He sees* FRAU HUBALEK.] What is it now? [*He takes a letter from her.*] Thank you, Frau Hubalek, thank you. [FRAU HUBALEK *leaves.*] Work in the Party, you say, and this very moment a letter comes from the Senate—would I be willing to take over next spring and so on, in recognition of my scientific achievements and so on, on condition that the Government and so on and so forth.

KROLEVSKY. Congratulations, Dr. Kürmann.

KÜRMANN. Thank you. [*He puts the letter down unopened on the desk.*] In recollection I always have the impression that you are smiling; yet when I look at you, you really never smile. No more than a chess player. Only you think you know my next move. You already see me as Professor H. Kürmann, Director of the Institute for Behavior Studies. [*Again the cracked piano next door, but only briefly.*] Tell me, Krolevsky, as a cyberneticist, do you think that the biography a man has is binding, the expression of an inevitable progression of events, or do you think that according to chance I might have had a quite different biography, and the biography one actually has, with all the given facts one is sick and tired of, is perhaps not even the most likely? Do you think our actual biography is merely one possible one, one of the many just as possible under the same social and historical conditions and with the same personal disposition? Looked at like that, what can a biography possibly tell us? It's not a question of a better or a worse biography, you understand. I merely refuse to attribute to everything that has happened—because it has happened, because it has become history and therefore irrevocable—a meaning which it doesn't possess.

KROLEVSKY. I understand.

KÜRMANN. You understand?

KROLEVSKY. *Ab posse ad esse valet, ab esse ad posse non valet.* [*He lights a cigarette.*] But I believe you had something urgent to tell me——

*Again the cracked piano from next door, but this time the exercise seems to be successful, so that it goes on. Five* BALLET PUPILS *dance out from the wings, followed by the* BALLET MASTER; *they are not dancing for the audience; it remains a practice.*

BALLET MASTER. Stop! What about the points? [*He demonstrates without the music.*] Got it? [*He claps his hands.*] Right, children, from the beginning!

*Again the cracked piano from next door. They repeat the exercise by dancing out into the wings. One* BALLET PUPIL *remains behind.*

*Silence.*

KÜRMANN. What's that girl doing here?

RECORDER. Do you like her?

KÜRMANN. I'm talking with Krolevsky.

RECORDER. You're talking with Krolevsky. Suddenly you're not listening to yourself; you look out of the window while you're speaking and see the ballet school next door. Suddenly you're rather absent-minded——

KÜRMANN. I don't know this ballet pupil.

RECORDER. But you could get to know her. [*The cracked piano is heard from next door, the three bars; the* BALLET PUPIL *performs the appropriate exercises; then silence again.*] That's how it was when you were talking with Krolevsky—about biographies.

KÜRMANN. Well?

RECORDER. You have permission to choose again, Herr Kürmann, to choose differently. Perhaps you would like to take her out to dinner——

*A* WAITER *appears with a menu.*

WAITER. What would you like, sir?

RECORDER. What is there?

WAITER. *Caviar russe. Saumon fumé. Foie gras de Strasbourg. Escargots à la bourguignonne.*

RECORDER. You can choose.

WAITER. Or Italian? *Cannelloni. Tortellini alla panna. Tortellini con funghi. Lasagne verdi.*

RECORDER. H'm.

WAITER. *Specialità della casa.*

RECORDER. An excellent restaurant, Herr Kürmann, and they don't know you here. [*To the* WAITER.] What fish have you?

WAITER. I'll show you. [*He goes out.*]

RECORDER. If you take the girl out to dinner, I can imagine that in four months, when Fräulein Dr. Stein comes from Paris, you will behave entirely differently, Herr Kürmann, with less constraint, more intellectually, more wittily, so that after two o'clock Fräulein Dr. Stein will take her handbag and leave. Biography without Antoinette. . . . [*The* WAITER *comes with a tray full of fish.*] Ah.

WAITER. Pike.

RECORDER. Look at this!

WAITER. Caught today.

RECORDER. Very fine.

WAITER. Sole. Whitefish. A very fine tench.

RECORDER. Enough for two?

WAITER. Oh yes.

RECORDER. Trout?

WAITER. We only have them alive.

RECORDER. What's that?

WAITER. *Spada.*

RECORDER. *Spada?*

WAITER. Swordfish.

RECORDER. Have you ever eaten swordfish?

WAITER. Absolutely fresh lobster.

KÜRMANN *looks at the* BALLET PUPIL.

RECORDER. Did you see the lobster? [*Again the cracked piano next door. The* BALLET PUPILS *dance out of the wings again, followed by the* BALLET MASTER, *and the girl who got separated takes her place in the group, which dances out. Silence.*] As you like. [*The* WAITER *is still holding the lobster.*] Perhaps another time.

WAITER. Thank you, sir. [*He leaves.*]

RECORDER. You see? You can choose.

KÜRMANN. Go on!

RECORDER. Why do you shout at me?

KÜRMANN. What do you take me for? As though it were a question of choosing a woman! If it's permissible, I'd rather have nothing to do with any woman at all.

RECORDER. As you like.

KROLEVSKY *is still sitting where he was.*

KROLEVSKY. Ab posse ad esse valet, ab esse ad posse non valet. [*He lights a cigarette.*] But I believe you had something urgent to tell me——

KÜRMANN *sits on the edge of the table.*

KÜRMANN. To come straight to the point, Krolevsky—you needn't answer me—you are a member of the Communist party, though up to now nobody has found out; at least an important link-man, probably one of the leaders. Your subject, mathematics, doesn't give you away. Your numerous trips, whether to Prague or Paris or Mexico City, are splendidly camouflaged by professional congresses. And you don't drink, so as not to spill the beans late in the night. [*He drinks.*] Let us suppose that one day it comes out and that on some pretext, at least in the name of the Philosophical Faculty, your continued membership of the teaching body were to be dispensed with, which would naturally rouse us, or some of us, to righteous indignation—suppression of academic freedom and so on. We should have the "Krolevsky Case" on our hands. I myself, as a nonconformist, should draft an appeal: "Dismayed by recent events at our University"—an appeal which would be as concerned as it was thoughtful, which it would be an honor to sign, and beyond that, of course, would not have the slightest effect.

KROLEVSKY. You speak from experience.

KÜRMANN. Certainly.

KROLEVSKY. Dr. Kürmann, what are you trying to tell me?

KÜRMANN. If we could begin again, we all know what we ought to do differently. Signatures for, signatures against, declarations, and the result is the powerlessness of the intelligentsia, of the opposition, force exercised in the name of the constitutional state, terrorization—the cost of never acting. [*To the* RECORDER.] When exactly did this conversation with Vladimir Krolevsky take place? [*The* RECORDER *leafs through the dossier.*] Soon afterward Professor Krolevsky was arrested, his house was searched, and he was dismissed from his chair.

RECORDER. 12/3/1959.

KÜRMANN. Add it to my dossier.

RECORDER. What?

KÜRMANN. 12/3/1959. Joined the Communist party.

*The* RECORDER *writes it down.*

KROLEVSKY. I confess, Dr. Kürmann, that you surprise me. The Party will examine your application. According to our inquiries, you have never belonged to any party. I hope you realize what it will mean to your academic career.

KÜRMANN. I realize very clearly what it means, Professor Krolevsky. That's why I'm doing it. [*To the* RECORDER, *who comes to* KÜRMANN *with the dossier.*] What am I to do?

RECORDER. Sign.

KÜRMANN *signs the dossier.*

KÜRMANN. Comrade Krolevsky—— [*Working light.*] What's the matter?

RECORDER. The doctor is waiting for you.

A STAGEHAND *brings a white armchair and puts it down in the foreground right; a second* STAGEHAND *wheels in an instrument trolley; then they both go.* KROLEVSKY *rises.*

KROLEVSKY. As far as we are concerned, Dr. Kürmann, our social relations will remain as before. An occasional little chat in the quadrangle of the University. Every now and then. We shall address one another by our official titles. [*He shakes hands.*] You know, Dr. Kürmann, that henceforth you will be kept under surveillance. [*He puts on his hat.*] If you give a party here in future, I shall not come to it.

KÜRMANN. Why a party?

KROLEVSKY. When you are made a professor in the very near future.

KÜRMANN. That will never happen!

*Acting light in the foreground. A* DOCTOR *in a white coat appears and holds a filmstrip up to the light.*

DOCTOR. Have you any pain?

KÜRMANN. Where?

DOCTOR. I'm asking you! Your EKG is fine. [*He gives* KÜRMANN *the filmstrip.*] Splendid. [*He goes to the instrument trolley.*] I'm not quite so happy about your urine.

KÜRMANN. Why?

DOCTOR. We shall see.

RECORDER. You must take off your jacket.

DOCTOR. We need a little blood.

> KÜRMANN *takes off his jacket.*

RECORDER. You can sit down.

> KÜRMANN *sits down and rolls up his sleeve.*

DOCTOR. Are you worried about anything? [*He inserts needle in* KÜRMANN'*s arm and extracts blood.*] What do you think about the Krolevsky case? [*He gives* KÜRMANN *a wad of cotton.*]

RECORDER. Hold the cotton on it.

> KÜRMANN *holds the cotton on it.*

KÜRMANN. I had mumps once when I was a child, and once I had measles, but apart from that . . .

> The DOCTOR *transfers the blood into a glass vessel.*

DOCTOR. Sister Agnes? [*He goes out.*]

KÜRMANN. What's the date today?

RECORDER. April 12, 1960. Fräulein Stein is still in Paris. She is packing her bag today to leave Paris. You can't alter that.

KÜRMANN. H'm.

RECORDER. She came with the guests who were celebrating your appointment as professor, but you did everything to prevent yourself from becoming a professor. [*Acting light in the room also. Two gentlemen in hats and coats appear, accompanied by* FRAU HUBALEK.] It seems to be working!

> The gentlemen look around.

FRAU HUBALEK. What can I do for you? Dr. Kürmann is not at home. I'm the housekeeper here. May I ask who you are?

> One of them shows a warrant.

RECORDER. Don't get up.

KÜRMANN. They're searching my flat?

RECORDER. You're at the doctor's. [KÜRMANN *sits down again*.] Keep the cotton on it. [*One of the men opens drawers*.] You're under suspicion of wanting to change the world. No one will ever suspect that you merely want to change your biography.

*The other man opens books.*

POLICEMAN. Frau——?

FRAU HUBALEK. Hubalek.

POLICEMAN. Tell me, Frau Hubalek——

FRAU HUBALEK. I know nothing.

POLICEMAN. Where do you come from?

FRAU HUBALEK. From Czechoslovakia.

POLICEMAN. From Czechoslovakia.

FRAU HUBALEK. What has the Doctor done?

POLICEMAN. You have relatives?

FRAU HUBALEK. In Czechoslovakia?

POLICEMAN. In Czechoslovakia.

FRAU HUBALEK. Why not?

POLICEMAN. Just answer the questions.

FRAU HUBALEK. He doesn't like his books to be touched.

POLICEMAN. How often do you visit your Czech relatives?

FRAU HUBALEK. Never.

POLICEMAN. That's not very often.

FRAU HUBALEK. It's enough for me.

*The* NURSE *appears in the foreground.*

NURSE. Doctor will be here in a minute. [*She takes something and goes away*.]

POLICEMAN. Tell me, Frau——

FRAU HUBALEK. Hubalek.

POLICEMAN. Are there any other rooms?

*The* POLICEMEN *and* FRAU HUBALEK *go out.*

RECORDER. They won't find anything, but don't worry: suspicion remains suspicion, and suspicion is enough.

*Room in darkness. In the foreground the* DOCTOR *comes back.*

DOCTOR. It's nothing serious. All the same, you must look after yourself. There's no joking with the liver. . . . Mind you, no *foie gras*, no *escargots à la bourguignonne*, nothing spiced. No pepper, mustard, curry. No seafood on any account——

*Neon lamp on.*

RECORDER. I'm making a note. [*He makes notes.*]

DOCTOR. No stone fruit: apricots, cherries, plums, peaches. No garlic. Nothing that causes flatulence. Cottage cheese whenever you like, as much cottage cheese as possible——

RECORDER. Vegetables?

DOCTOR. Yes, but without salt. Apart from cabbage. No French beans, in fact no beans at all, no onions——

RECORDER. Nothing that causes flatulence.

DOCTOR. Nothing cold. No beer. No whisky and vodka and so on, no gin, kirsch, pear brandy, and so on, Steinhäger, grappa, marc, and so on, cognac, calvados and so on. Under no circumstances.

RECORDER. Wine?

DOCTOR. You say your father used to drink?

KÜRMANN. So it seems.

DOCTOR. Above all, no white wine.

RECORDER. How about red wine?

DOCTOR. No alcohol at all.

RECORDER. What can he drink then?

DOCTOR. Milk.

RECORDER. Mineral water?

DOCTOR. But not carbonated. Tea. But no strong tea, of course. And then camomile, linden blossom, peppermint, rosehip, and so on. Absolutely no coffee. Do you like yogurt?

RECORDER. Do you like yogurt?

DOCTOR. Yogurt whenever you like. As much cottage cheese as possible. Vegetables whenever you like, but without salt. No seafood on any account——

RECORDER. We've had that.

DOCTOR. I'll tell you one thing you can eat: blue trout.

RECORDER. That's something.

DOCTOR. Without butter.

RECORDER. Lobster?

DOCTOR. For heaven's sake!

RECORDER. You've been lucky. Herr Kürmann very nearly had a lobster the other day.

DOCTOR. For heaven's sake!

RECORDER. Meat?

DOCTOR. Boiled. That's perfectly all right. Without fat. Nothing stewed. Boiled or grilled. Without salt. Without spices, as I said. No sausages and so on——

RECORDER. Bread?

DOCTOR. Crispbread.

RECORDER. Nothing that causes flatulence.

DOCTOR. As much cottage cheese as possible. [*The* NURSE *enters.*] I'm coming.

*The* NURSE *wheels the instrument trolley away.*

RECORDER. Anything else?

DOCTOR. Sweat. Sweat as much as you can.

RECORDER. How?

DOCTOR. Sport, walking, sauna. [*He puts his hand on* KÜRMANN's *shoulder.*] It's nothing serious, a slight enlargement of the liver; apart from that, I found absolutely nothing. The most important thing of all, my dear sir, is no excitement, no excitement of any kind. . . .

*Working light. The whole stage is visible again; a number of people are gathered in the background, gentlemen in dinner jackets, ladies in evening dress, all with champagne glasses in their hands. The* DOCTOR *has gone.*

KÜRMANN. Not a word about cancer.

RECORDER. No.

KÜRMANN. Apart from that, he didn't find anything.

RECORDER. You can put your jacket on again.

KÜRMANN. As much cottage cheese as possible. . . .

RECORDER. What are you thinking about?

KÜRMANN *rises and takes his jacket.*

KÜRMANN. Who are these people?

RECORDER. Friends.

KÜRMANN. What do they want?

RECORDER. They've come to celebrate with you.

KÜRMANN. What for?

RECORDER. You've been made a professor.

*Acting light in the room. The room is full of* GUESTS; *they are standing in groups, chatting; it is impossible to make out a word.*

KÜRMANN. Professor?

RECORDER. Quite frankly, I'm surprised.

KÜRMANN. A member of the Communist party doesn't get made a professor in this country in 1960. That's impossible.

RECORDER. Unlikely.

KÜRMANN *shakes his head.*

HENRIK. Hannes!

RECORDER. They're calling you.

HENRIK. Where has he got to?

KÜRMANN *shakes his head.*

RECORDER. The guests want to go. It's late. [*He helps* KÜRMANN *into his jacket.*] That's something I don't have to explain to you, Professor Kürmann; no system guarantees that the probable will happen in every case.

KÜRMANN *is discovered.*

HENRIK. There you are.

SCHNEIDER. It's two o'clock.

HENRIK. We're leaving you now, Professor.

KÜRMANN *disappears among the* GUESTS; *a buzz of voices;* GUESTS *leave the room in groups, until only the young lady in the evening dress is left exactly as in the beginning; she is sitting in the easy chair, waiting; she is wearing the horn-rimmed spectacles. Voices of the departing* GUESTS *outside; soon afterward* KÜRMANN *comes back —without whistling.*

ANTOINETTE. "I'm going soon too."

*Pause.*

KÜRMANN. "Don't you feel well?"

ANTOINETTE. "On the contrary." [*She takes a cigarette.*] "Just one more cigarette." [*She waits in vain for a light and lights up for herself.*] "If I'm not in the way." [*She smokes.*] "I enjoyed it very much. Some of them were very nice, I thought, very stimulating. . . ." [*Pause.*] "Have you anything left to drink?" [KÜRMANN *does not move.*] "Why are you looking at me like that?"

*Silence.*

# PART TWO

*Acting light. The room in the morning;* FRAU HUBALEK *is clearing up; after a while* KÜRMANN *enters in a dressing gown, carrying letters.*

KÜRMANN. Frau Hubalek—good morning—would you be so kind as to make breakfast, Frau Hubalek. [*He stands and opens letters.*] I asked if you would be so kind as to make breakfast, Frau Hubalek. [*She exits.*] I know exactly what you're thinking now. But you're wrong. You're thinking I would always do the same thing, even if I could start afresh a hundred times over. [*He reads a letter and throws it into the wastepaper basket.*] Congratulations! [*He throws the whole bundle into the wastepaper basket.*] But you're wrong. We shan't drive out into the country. We shan't get to know each other. [*He sits down at the desk.*] It will be our first and last breakfast.

RECORDER. As you like.

KÜRMANN. We shan't become a couple.

RECORDER. You still have the choice.

ANTOINETTE *appears in an evening dress; she remains by the door, so that* KÜRMANN *does not notice her.*

KÜRMANN. What day of the week is it?

RECORDER. Thursday. [KÜRMANN *looks at his wrist watch.*] You have a meeting at eleven, remember, a meeting you missed——

*The cracked piano is heard again from next door, the three bars, interrupted.* KÜRMANN *sees* ANTOINETTE *and rises.*

ANTOINETTE. I borrowed your toothbrush.

KÜRMANN. I forgot to ask: coffee or tea? Perhaps you'd rather have coffee. [*He goes to the door.*] And a soft-boiled egg?

ANTOINETTE. Not for me. [*Pause; they stand.*] What time is it?

KÜRMANN. I've got a meeting at eleven.

ANTOINETTE *hunts through her handbag.*

ANTOINETTE. If only I knew where I parked my car. I've got the key. [*She ponders.*] An avenue, is that possible? An avenue with a monument. . . .

KÜRMANN. There's no avenue here.

ANTOINETTE. Funny.

KÜRMANN. Why don't we sit down? [FRAU HUBALEK *enters and sets the table; the two stand and wait until she has gone.*] Our tea will be here in a minute.

ANTOINETTE. Now I remember where I left my car! [*She laughs.*] I'm always surprised when I manage to find my car. [*Casually.*] Do you know young Stahel?

KÜRMANN. Stahel?

ANTOINETTE. He drove my car. He didn't want to come up. And the avenue was earlier on. . . . [*A clock strikes ten.*] Ten o'clock? [*She takes the jacket of her evening dress from the armchair.*]

KÜRMANN. Are you going already?

ANTOINETTE. If you don't mind, Hannes.

KÜRMANN. Without breakfast?

ANTOINETTE. I've got to work, too. Ten o'clock! I have to change. My God, I had an appointment for ten! [KÜRMANN *watches as she puts on her jacket.*] Don't worry.

KÜRMANN. Why are you laughing?

ANTOINETTE. The way men do worry. I don't sleep with many men, but every time I do, I'm always glad afterward to be by myself again, just the same as you are, Hannes. Where on earth did I put my watch?

KÜRMANN. In the bathroom, I think. [ANTOINETTE *goes into the bathroom.*] Is that how it was?

RECORDER. Exactly like that.

KÜRMANN. Not a word about meeting again?

RECORDER. Not a word.

KÜRMANN. I don't understand.

RECORDER. According to the dossier [*Neon lamp on; he refers to the dossier.*], she comes out of the bathroom, but dressed and with her hair combed. She immediately looks for her car key; the clock strikes ten; she takes her jacket; not a word about seeing you again. Your memory has invented things, Herr Kürmann. She doesn't sit on your left or your right knee; she doesn't put her arm around your neck; she doesn't give you a kiss that forces you to indulge in prolonged caresses. Nothing of the sort. She has an appointment too. She doesn't seem either disappointed or confused. On the contrary, she obviously enjoyed the night, but what's over is over;

she doesn't even keep to the intimate way you addressed each other during the night.

KÜRMANN. I don't understand——

RECORDER. That's how it was, Herr Kürmann.

KÜRMANN. Why did I miss the meeting? [*Neon lamp off.*] What is she doing all this time?

RECORDER. She's looking for her watch.

*Pause.* ANTOINETTE *comes back; she is putting on her watch.*

ANTOINETTE. I'm going to have another look at the rooms today— you know, for my gallery. Unfortunately, there's no elevator in the building. That's the only snag, but the rooms would be splendid. Exactly what I'm looking for. Big and plain. Unfortunately, they're very expensive. I should have to have a skylight put in. That's why I'm meeting this young architect today.

RECORDER. Stahel.

ANTOINETTE. To find out how much it would cost. The position is unique, and if the gallery is a success, I shall take the flat underneath and start my little publishing firm. Later on. And if it doesn't work out, I shall go back to Paris. That will be decided today. . . .

*Pause.*

RECORDER. All you need do is take her to the elevator.

ANTOINETTE. Yes.

KÜRMANN. Let's hope it works out—I mean the skylight.

ANTOINETTE. Yes.

KÜRMANN. Yes.

ANTOINETTE. Keep your fingers crossed for me!

KÜRMANN *goes out with her;* FRAU HUBALEK *brings the tea and leaves again; then* KÜRMANN *comes back.*

KÜRMANN. An unusual woman.

RECORDER. You see.

KÜRMANN. A magnificent woman.

RECORDER. You underestimated her; at the time you didn't want to believe that after sleeping with you, a woman too might want to be alone.

KÜRMANN. A unique woman.

*Neon lamp on.*

RECORDER. As far as the meeting at eleven is concerned, you will remember: [*He reads from the dossier.*] "Item One: election of a new rector of the University." [KÜRMANN *walks over to the window.*] It might be important, Herr Kürmann, and not only for you personally, but for you as well, that your colleague Hornacher should not be elected. Hornacher, as everyone knows, is a virulent anti-Communist, insignificant as a scholar, but a man of strong views. A man concerned with the spiritual defense of the nation. If Hornacher were elected rector, he would leave no stone unturned to see that you, Herr Kürmann, lose your job. That too will be decided today. . . . Are you listening? . . . In the first version of your biography you missed today's session because you thought you had to drive out into the country with the young lady to eat fish and drink the local wine. Hornacher was elected, though by a very small majority. Then you regretted missing the meeting. Do you remember? And yet Hornacher could do you no harm in the first version because you were not a member of the Communist party.

KÜRMANN. Why doesn't she drive off? [*Pause.*] She isn't driving off.

RECORDER. Perhaps it's because of the battery. You know what it's like: she leaves the parking lights on all night; then she wonders why the starter doesn't work. Or she can see you standing at the window. [KÜRMANN *leaves the window.*] What are you thinking about?

KÜRMANN *pours a cup of tea.*

KÜRMANN. I underestimated her.

RECORDER. Who doubts that?

KÜRMANN *stands drinking tea.*

KÜRMANN. What is she going to do now?

RECORDER. See that she is never underestimated again. [KÜRMANN *drinks tea.*] Your wife has our unqualified admiration, believe me, our unqualified admiration. If I may say so, she is superior to you. Don't worry about what she will do now. A woman of her intelligence will make her way in life without you, Herr Kürmann. Have no fear. She knows what she wants. She is a woman, but more than that: a personality, but more than that: a woman.

KÜRMANN. Oh, yes.

RECORDER. She will run a gallery, "Antoinette Gallery," or a small publishing firm, "Antoinette Editions," and if that doesn't work out, she can go back to Paris at any time.

KÜRMANN. To her dancer.

RECORDER. Now she is meeting a young architect to find out what a skylight costs. Perhaps it will be too expensive, but the young architect will know how to appreciate her, a woman full of plans and independent, and one day, who knows, she may have a child that brings all her plans to nothing; but all that need not bother you, Herr Kürmann—she has gone.

KÜRMANN. Yes.

RECORDER. Worry about the Institute instead. [KÜRMANN *sits down at the desk.*] What you are holding in your hands is a document which you are supposed to place before today's meeting, a photocopy concerning Horst Dieter Hornacher, who is to be elected rector today: his signature in 1941. [KÜRMANN *skims through the document.*] It's time you got dressed if you don't want to miss today's meeting again. [*He looks at his watch, then at* KÜRMANN.] Ten-thirty . . .

KÜRMANN. Can we go back again?

RECORDER. Why?

KÜRMANN. I underestimated that woman.

RECORDER. You will underestimate her again.

KÜRMANN. What do you mean?

RECORDER. As you wish. [*Neon lamp off;* ANTOINETTE *comes back.*] Herr Kürmann wants to go back again.

KÜRMANN *takes off her horn-rimmed spectacles.*

ANTOINETTE. What for?

KÜRMANN. I'm not going to let you go.

ANTOINETTE. You've got a meeting.

KÜRMANN. Seriously.

ANTOINETTE. Seriously.

KÜRMANN. We don't know one another.

ANTOINETTE. That's the nice thing about it.

KÜRMANN. Why are you laughing?

ANTOINETTE. Do you need a declaration of love next morning? [*Pause.*] Give me my glasses.

KÜRMANN. I've got a suggestion to make. I'll skip the meeting, although it's very important, and you skip this architect with his skylight, and we'll drive out into the country; we'll drive out at random.

ANTOINETTE. Out into nature?

KÜRMANN. It's a marvelous day.

ANTOINETTE. Hand in hand through the rushes?

KÜRMANN. We needn't walk, we needn't roam through the rushes; we'll sit down at an inn by the lake; we'll eat fish with a light local wine; the whole thing need not be in bad taste. [*She smiles.*] Antoinette, please! [*He gives her back her horn-rimmed spectacles.*]

ANTOINETTE. "Where on earth did I put my watch?"

KÜRMANN. "In the bathroom, I think."

ANTOINETTE *goes into the bathroom.*

RECORDER. So you want the first version after all! [*Neon lamp on.*] You know what follows. [*He reads from the dossier.*] "Lunch in the Swan Hotel, discussion about General de Gaulle. / Evening alone; news that Hornacher was elected rector. / Saturday morning: Fräulein Stein is spending the weekend with her parents. Monday in the Institute; later an aperitif in town; evening both busy, but a phone call after midnight: the skylight is prohibitive."

KÜRMANN. And so on!

RECORDER. "Wednesday: Antoinette flies to Paris; you promise in the airport bar that you will never write to each other. / Friday: Lecture at the Philosophical Society, Behavior Studies and Anthropology. / Weekend together in Paris, Hotel Port Royal."

KÜRMANN. And so on and so forth!

RECORDER. "She is a secretary at Gallimard."

KÜRMANN. For whose benefit are you reading that out?

RECORDER. And so on. [*He leafs through but does not read anything out.*] Happiness, trip to Greece, happiness, abortion, happiness. . . . [*He takes a card from the dossier.*] "We marry. Antoinette Stein, Hannes Kürmann, June 1961." [KÜRMANN *fills his pipe.*] So you want that to stand. . . . You still have a choice—you want breakfast together?

KÜRMANN. Yes.

*The* RECORDER *makes a note in the dossier.*

RECORDER. "Breakfast together."

*The sound of a crash from outside in the street.*

KÜRMANN. What was that?

RECORDER. That doesn't count.

KÜRMANN. An accident?

RECORDER. That would also have been possible. [*He takes a slip of paper.*] "5/27. Time: 10:17. An Austin-Cooper bearing license plate 907 139 was struck by the trailer of a lorry as it emerged from the car park——"

KÜRMANN. Antoinette!

RECORDER. She evidently didn't look in the rear-view mirror.

KÜRMANN. Dead?

RECORDER. Pull yourself together.

KÜRMANN. Dead?

RECORDER. Cuts on the face. [*He crumples up the slip of paper.*] But that doesn't count, Herr Kürmann. Fortunately we've recorded "Breakfast together." [*The sirens of an ambulance.*] Stop!

*Working light. The whole stage is visible; silence; in the background AMBULANCE MEN are standing with a stretcher.*

RECORDER. We're sticking to the first version.

*The AMBULANCE MEN leave.*

*Acting light. The room as before.*

RECORDER. Go on. [ANTOINETTE *comes back from the bathroom.*] Go on! The tea is there. . . . [KÜRMANN *and* ANTOINETTE *remain standing.*] Why don't you sit down?

KÜRMANN. Do we have to repeat everything now—even what we don't want to alter: Hotel Port Royal—including happiness and everything? . . . That's impossible.

ANTOINETTE. No.

KÜRMANN. The joy, the anticipation, the way she stood there on the Gare de l'Est. And all our conversations, our happy conversations. . . . How can we repeat that when the secrets have been exhausted? When the uncertainty has been exhausted, the pull of anticipation from moment to moment. . . . Can you imagine it:

that morning in Salonica and the way we stood on that little ship along with the stinking sheep? My jokes, her jokes—how on earth are we to laugh at them again?

ANTOINETTE. Can't we skip that?

KÜRMANN. Can't we skip that?

RECORDER. Skip the joy?

KÜRMANN. Yes.

ANTOINETTE. Yes.

KÜRMANN. Just you try repeating a joy when you know what follows it!

*Neon lamp on.*

RECORDER. Then what do you want to change? [*He leafs this way and that through the dossier.*] The abortion? [KÜRMANN *and* ANTOINETTE *look at each other; for a moment they hesitate, then both shake their heads.*] What then? [*The* RECORDER *continues leafing through the dossier.*]

KÜRMANN. I know what I should like to change.

RECORDER. What?

KÜRMANN. June 2, 1963.

ANTOINETTE. What happened then?

RECORDER. 1963, June——

KÜRMANN. The morning.

*The* RECORDER *searches through the dossier until he finds the page.*

RECORDER. The slap in the face? [KÜRMANN *nods.*] All right. [*Neon lamp off.*] It is nine in the morning, Frau Kürmann. You're not at home yet; we don't know where you are at this moment. [AN-TOINETTE *goes out.*] Go ahead. [KÜRMANN *now lights the pipe he has filled.*] 1963. [*The* RECORDER *reads from the dossier.*] "President Kennedy visits West Berlin. / Earthquake in Libya. / Fidel Castro is the first foreigner to be named a Hero of the Soviet Union——"

KÜRMANN. This isn't my tobacco.

RECORDER. Why not?

KÜRMANN. It's a ghastly tobacco.

RECORDER. But cheap. [KÜRMANN *taps out his pipe.*] That's what comes of not having a steady income any longer, Herr Kür-mann——

KÜRMANN. Why not? [*A gentleman in a dignified overcoat, homburg in hand, is standing in the room as though a longish conversation had already taken place.* KÜRMANN *is standing with his hands in the pockets of his dressing gown.*] I understand, Magnificence, I understand.

HORNACHER. I apologize for disturbing you at breakfast. But I felt compelled by the dictates of correct behavior not to approach the Senate in this matter before I had once more made personal inquiries. [*Pause.*] I am waiting for a clear answer.

KÜRMANN. Magnificence, I am a member of the Communist party. I believe in the aims of the Communist party insofar as it stands for Marxism-Leninism, and I beg the Senate to take appropriate action.

HORNACHER *puts on his homburg.*

RECORDER. Wait!

HORNACHER. A clear answer.

RECORDER. Perhaps Herr Professor Kürmann, after listening to himself, might like to answer differently. [*To* KÜRMANN.] Perhaps this answer seems to you too simple. Or too heroic.

HORNACHER *takes off his homburg.*

KÜRMANN. Magnificence——

HORNACHER. Well?

KÜRMANN. I don't believe in Marxism-Leninism. Which of course doesn't mean that I consider the Russian Revolution a misfortune. On the contrary, I don't believe in Marxism-Leninism as a doctrine of eternal salvation. That's what I wanted to say. But nor do I believe in your Christian doctrine of salvation by free enterprise, whose history we know by now. I believe in that even less. It's difficult, Magnificence. I consider that the alternatives imposed upon us at the present time are out of date, which means they're wrong. But since they are imposed upon us, I shall remain a member of the Communist party so long as I live in the West. I choose the restriction of freedom that doesn't benefit merely the practitioners of free enterprise. I confess that I don't consider the USSR to be paradise. Otherwise I should go there. But I deny the West any right to a crusade. . . . That's enough, I should think. . . .

HORNACHER. I should think so too.

Kürmann. And yet that answer isn't right either. It's true that my entry into the Party in December 1959 was not unconsidered, but fundamentally it was—how shall I say?—a private and personal act. I expected consequences; they don't surprise me. In fact I expected them sooner. [*He laughs, then once more addresses* Hornacher *in official terms.*] I thank you for the discussion, Magnificence, and beg the Senate to take appropriate action.

Hornacher *puts on his homburg.*

Recorder. Wait!

Kürmann. Was the first answer better?

Recorder. Briefer.

Kürmann. Let's take the first.

Hornacher. A clear answer.

Kürmann. If you value clarity, I can answer even more clearly. [*He looks for something.*] One moment.

Recorder. Take off your hat again.

Hornacher *takes off his homburg.*

Kürmann. I have here a photocopy which the Senate, I will charitably suppose, knows nothing about: your signature in 1941. [*He rises and gives* Hornacher *the photocopy.*] You saw to it that someone who might possibly have stood in the way of your academic career was deported in 1941, along with his family, for the protection of the Fatherland. [Hornacher *returns the document.*] You will say it's a forgery.

Hornacher. Yes.

Kürmann. Then prove it.

Hornacher. You're mistaken. I don't have to prove anything. It's you who have to prove something, and you're hardly likely to do that with a photocopy provided by the Communist party. Your source is unreliable.

Kürmann. And therefore I am unacceptable.

Hornacher. I'm afraid so. [Kürmann *puts the photocopy back in the desk.*] Can I put my hat on now?

Recorder. Wait!

Kürmann. Magnificence, you're a swine, and a university that elects you its rector . . .

*Pause.*

RECORDER. Which of the three answers do you want?

HORNACHER. The effect remains the same.

KÜRMANN. Let him take all three. [HORNACHER *puts on his hom-burg.*] That's to say—no. He doesn't need to know that this photo-copy exists. . . . The first one.

RECORDER. Magnificence, the first answer stands.

HORNACHER *leaves.*

*Neon lamp on.*

RECORDER. That was 1962.

KÜRMANN. I shall emigrate.

RECORDER. It's now 1963. You haven't emigrated.

FRAU HUBALEK *comes in with the mail.*

KÜRMANN. Is my wife back?

FRAU HUBALEK. No.

KÜRMANN. Thank you, Frau Hubalek, thank you. [FRAU HUBALEK *goes.*] I haven't emigrated. . . .

RECORDER. No.

KÜRMANN. I'm standing here in this dressing gown again, and I've been waiting all night to see whether she comes home, when she comes home, how she comes home. [*He laughs.*] Exactly like that.

RECORDER. Differently.

KÜRMANN. Now it's ten in the morning.

RECORDER. In the first version you didn't laugh, Herr Kürmann; you were worried.

KÜRMANN *goes to the telephone and dials a number.*

KÜRMANN. Hello. . . . Hello——

RECORDER. Why don't you speak?

KÜRMANN. There's always this crackling noise.

RECORDER. That needn't stop you speaking.

KÜRMANN. Why does it always crackle like that?

RECORDER. Your phone is being tapped. [KÜRMANN *puts down the receiver.*] Something has already changed. . . .

STAGEHANDS *bring a spinet.*

KÜRMANN. What's that?

RECORDER. A spinet; because Antoinette, as it suddenly turned out, is musical. Do you remember?

*The* STAGEHANDS *go out.*

KÜRMANN. What else has changed?

RECORDER. There's no more whisky in the house. In the first version, you remember, you drank rather a lot when you waited for Antoinette. And at other times. The doctor convinced you that your liver was in danger. You feel better than in the first version.

KÜRMANN *listens.*

KÜRMANN. At last!

*Neon lamp off.*

KÜRMANN *sits down at the desk.* ANTOINETTE *enters in a different evening dress; her hair is done in a style that makes her look younger than before.*

ANTOINETTE. My apologies. [*Pause; she sits down to breakfast.*] The Schneiders send their regards.

KÜRMANN. The tea is cold.

ANTOINETTE. Everyone thought it was a pity you hadn't come. [*She pours tea.*] I enjoyed it very much. Some of them were very nice, I thought, very stimulating. [*She drinks.*] The Schneiders send their regards——

KÜRMANN. You've already said that.

ANTOINETTE. Have you had breakfast already?

KÜRMANN. It's ten o'clock. [*He pretends to be working.*]

*Pause.*

ANTOINETTE. Henrik sends his regards too.

KÜRMANN. Who?

ANTOINETTE. Henrik.

KÜRMANN. That surprises me.

ANTOINETTE. Why does that surprise you?

KÜRMANN. Because Henrik is in London at the moment.

*She turns around and looks at him.*

ANTOINETTE. Hannes—what's wrong?

KÜRMANN. I'm asking you.

ANTOINETTE. I come home——

KÜRMANN. ——at ten in the morning.

ANTOINETTE. I give you regards from Henrik——

KÜRMANN. ——who is in London at the moment.

ANTOINETTE. You mean I'm lying? [*She nonchalantly takes a ciga-rette.*] Henrik is not in London.

KÜRMANN *jumps up.*

RECORDER. That has changed. This time Henrik hasn't flown to London; this time it isn't a lie; this time you're in the wrong.

KÜRMANN. Sorry. [*He goes over and gives her a light.*]

ANTOINETTE. Have your proofs arrived?

*She sits smoking;* KÜRMANN *stands.*

KÜRMANN. Who else sends his regards?

RECORDER. She means the proofs of a paperback you are now writing for the Rowohlt Verlag: *Behavior Studies for Everyman.* As I said, you've no steady income any more, no institute at which to carry out research. You have to be glad of any job you can get. That's new.

KÜRMANN. The proofs have arrived. [*A clock strikes ten.*] Where's your wrist watch? [*She looks at her bare wrist.*] In a bathroom?

FRAU HUBALEK *comes in.*

FRAU HUBALEK. Frau Doktor?

ANTOINETTE. What is it?

FRAU HUBALEK. Shall I make some fresh tea? [*She takes the pot and goes out.*]

ANTOINETTE. I should like to know what you really imagine. We've been married for two years now; I translate from morning till night, and if I don't go out and meet people, I shall never get a gallery. You say that yourself. But every time I come from a party, you look to see whether I've got my watch. What is really on your mind?

KÜRMANN. You tell me.

ANTOINETTE. What?

KÜRMANN. Where you've been.

*She stubs out her cigarette.*

ANTOINETTE. If you want to know——

*Neon lamp on.*

RECORDER. Do you want to know? Originally you reacted very badly to certainty. [*He looks it up in the dossier.*] You shouted. First you smashed a teacup, then you shouted. Not for long though; after that you became solemn. When Antoinette—for her part nonchalance in person—pointed out that you were behaving like a boor, you slapped her face, to your own amazement: once on the left, and because she couldn't believe it, twice on the right. Then, in order not to look at Antoinette, you banged your fist on the spinet; meanwhile, according to the dossier, the following words were uttered. [KÜRMANN *makes a dismissive gesture with his hand.*] Do you really want to know for sure?

KÜRMANN. Yes.

RECORDER. As you like.

*Neon lamp off.*

ANTOINETTE. If you want me to, Hannes, I'll go. And right away. I'm not living in the nineteenth century. I'm not going to put up with that.

KÜRMANN. I was only joking about the watch.

ANTOINETTE. When you're white in the face, you're not joking.

KÜRMANN. Then I'm sorry.

ANTOINETTE. I'm not going to let myself be shouted at by a man.

KÜRMANN. I haven't shouted.

ANTOINETTE. Because you know I'd go if you did.

KÜRMANN *takes an empty teacup.*

KÜRMANN. Did I shout in any way?

RECORDER. No.

KÜRMANN. Record that!

*Neon lamp on. The* RECORDER *records. Neon lamp off.*

ANTOINETTE. You say nothing because you know how cheap what you're thinking is. Nevertheless you're thinking it. [*She becomes vehement.*] I think it's mean.

KÜRMANN. What is?

ANTOINETTE. The way you treat me.

KÜRMANN. For instance?

ANTOINETTE. Go on, shout at me! So Frau Hubalek can hear! Go on, show what kind of man you are! Go on, slap my face!

KÜRMANN. Why?

ANTOINETTE. Like the boor you are!

FRAU HUBALEK *comes in with the tea.*

KÜRMANN. Thank you, Frau Hubalek, thank you.

FRAU HUBALEK *goes out.*

ANTOINETTE. We've been married two years and it's the first time I've stayed out all night, the first time, and every time you make a scene——

KÜRMANN. Antoinette.

ANTOINETTE. Every time!

KÜRMANN *stirs his empty cup.*

KÜRMANN. You're making a scene, Antoinette, not me. What am I doing? I'm standing here drinking tea.

ANTOINETTE. Tea?

KÜRMANN. Tea.

ANTOINETTE. From an empty cup.

*Pause.*

KÜRMANN. Why is she crying now?

*Neon lamp on.*

RECORDER. That's right, in the first version she didn't cry. Because you shouted, Herr Kürmann, in the first version. Now she's crying. It's impossible for both parts of a couple to be superior at the same time. This time it's you.

*Neon lamp off.*

ANTOINETTE. Fancy having to put up with that. I think it's mean. [*She yells.*] Mean—mean—mean!

KÜRMANN. What is?

ANTOINETTE. The way you have to control yourself.

KÜRMANN *stirs his empty cup.*

KÜRMANN. Now you're really acting as though I'd slapped your face,

Antoinette. [*To the* RECORDER.] Did I slap her face?

RECORDER. No.

KÜRMANN. Record that! [*Neon lamp on. The* RECORDER *records. Neon lamp off.*] I was worried. I was working. Reading the proofs. I rang up. At two in the morning. The Schneiders were already in bed. You had gone, they told me——

> *She takes something out of her handbag.*

ANTOINETTE. Here's my watch. [KÜRMANN *goes across and fills his teacup.*] I can only tell you, you're wrong.

KÜRMANN. Then it's all right.

ANTOINETTE. It's not all right at all, Hannes. I think it's incredible, a man like you, an intellectual, a man of your age—I mean a man of your experience—have you nothing else in the world to think about except whether I've slept with someone or not? Is that your only problem? [*She stands up.*] And just supposing I had slept with a man last night, or every time you imagined it—so what? I ask you: so what? Would that be the nuclear destruction of the world?

KÜRMANN. Now you're talking nonsense.

ANTOINETTE. I did sleep with someone.

> *Pause.*

KÜRMANN. Would you like some more tea?

> *She takes her handbag.*

ANTOINETTE. I have to change now.

KÜRMANN. Do that.

ANTOINETTE. I've got a date for lunch. [*She goes out.*]

RECORDER. Now you know. [*Neon lamp on.*] You didn't shout, Herr Kürmann, not in the least. Nor did you slap her face, although Antoinette was waiting for it. And the spinet is undamaged too. You behaved like an experienced man—irreproachably.

KÜRMANN. And what difference does that make?

RECORDER. Perfectly.

KÜRMANN. The facts remain the same.

RECORDER. But you feel superior. [KÜRMANN *smashes the cup on the bookcase.*] You know what follows——

KÜRMANN. She met him for lunch. She wouldn't tell me his name. That was none of my business, she said. A month later they went to Sicily together.

RECORDER. Sardinia. [*The telephone rings.*] Aren't you going to answer?

KÜRMANN. No. [*He lets it ring.*] Wrong number.

RECORDER. How do you know?

KÜRMANN. As soon as he hears my voice: wrong number. I've been through that before. We won't repeat it.

ANTOINETTE *comes in wearing her coat.*

ANTOINETTE. I'm going now, Hannes.

KÜRMANN. Where to?

ANTOINETTE. To town.

KÜRMANN. To town.

ANTOINETTE. I told you I had a lunch date. I'll be spending the afternoon in the library. I'll be back in the evening.

*Pause. She puts her gloves on.*

RECORDER. Here, in this position, you apologized for everything: for slapping her face, smashing the spinet, for everything. But that's no longer necessary. . . .

*Pause, until* ANTOINETTE *has finished putting her gloves on.*

KÜRMANN. May I ask what his name is?

ANTOINETTE. I want you to leave me in peace now. That's all I can tell you. This is my affair. [*She takes her handbag.*] If anything changes between us, Hannes, I'll tell you. [*She leaves.*]

RECORDER. Did you expect anything else?

KÜRMANN. Go on!

RECORDER. She doesn't tell you—even without a slap in the face. To that extent, your irreproachable behavior has changed nothing, but you feel better than in the first version. This time you've nothing to feel ashamed of.

KÜRMANN. Go on!

RECORDER. Don't you feel better?

FRAU HUBALEK *brings the mail.*

KÜRMANN. Thank you, Frau Hubalek, thank you.

FRAU HUBALEK *clears away the breakfast things.*

RECORDER. That's a week later. There would be that letter to Antoinette again, which you opened to find out where you stood. You remember? After that she rented a P.O. box.

KÜRMANN *eyes the letter.*

KÜRMANN. Frau Hubalek!

RECORDER. That was when you started behaving in a way that wasn't worthy of you——

KÜRMANN. A special delivery letter for my wife.

KÜRMANN *gives her the letter;* FRAU HUBALEK *goes out.*

RECORDER. You see, you can act differently.

KÜRMANN. Go on!

RECORDER. Your behavior is beyond reproach.

KÜRMANN. What happens in a month?

RECORDER. Antoinette will be grateful to you. Antoinette will respect you. She may take a P. O. box just the same, but not because she doesn't trust you. For reasons of tact——

KÜRMANN. I asked, what happens in a month?

RECORDER. Summer 1963. [*He looks it up in the dossier.*] "Konrad Adenauer considers retiring——"

KÜRMANN. Here, I mean, what happens here?

RECORDER. You're still living together.

ANTOINETTE *comes in wearing a coat and carrying a small suitcase, which she puts down in order to put on her gloves. Neon lamp off.*

ANTOINETTE. I'm going now, Hannes.

KÜRMANN. Have you got everything?

ANTOINETTE. I'll be back in a week.

KÜRMANN. Have you got your passport?

ANTOINETTE. In a week at the latest. [*She looks in her handbag for her passport.*]

KÜRMANN. Drive carefully. I've been reading the weather forecast: the Gotthard is open, but Italy reports floods, especially on the Via Aurelia——

ANTOINETTE. We're flying.

KÜRMANN. Has that been changed?

RECORDER. Evidently.

ANTOINETTE. We've changed our minds. We're flying.

KÜRMANN. I'm relieved to hear it.

ANTOINETTE. Egon only has a week free.

*Pause.*

KÜRMANN. How about your mail?

ANTOINETTE. Frau Hubalek has the housekeeping money.

KÜRMANN. When does your plane leave?

ANTOINETTE. At one o'clock. [KÜRMANN *looks at his watch.*] You needn't forward the mail. There won't be anything important, and I shall be back in a week, Hannes—by Monday or Tuesday at the latest. . . . [*Pause.*] What are you going to do?

KÜRMANN. Correct proofs. . . . [ANTOINETTE *picks up her little suitcase.*] You've got plenty of time, Antoinette, plenty. It will only take you forty minutes to get to the airport. At the outside. It's only ten now. Not even that. [*To the* RECORDER.] Why is she so jumpy?

RECORDER. You're behaving so perfectly, and Antoinette didn't count on that. In the first version there was an hour-long argument at this point. You had to confess that you had opened a letter. Antoinette was beside herself. You had to confess seven times over and pacify her and beg forgiveness, until finally she could take her suitcase and go——

KÜRMANN. She will get to the airport far too early.

RECORDER. Because there's nothing to forgive.

*A clock strikes ten.*

ANTOINETTE. Hannes, I must go. [*She gives him a kiss.*]

KÜRMANN. Drive carefully—I mean, fly carefully. . . . [ANTOINETTE *leaves.*] His name is Egon.

RECORDER. His personal particulars remain unchanged. [*Neon lamp on.*] "Stahel, Egon. Born 1929. Architect. Married. Catholic."

KÜRMANN. Stahel.

RECORDER. You heard the name three years ago, but you took no notice of it. Now you hear it wherever you go. People who don't know anything yet, especially, keep mentioning the name all the time: Egon or Stahel. The young man seems to be very highly thought of. As an architect. But also as a man and as a musician. [KÜRMANN *goes to the liquor cabinet.*] There's no more whisky in the house. I've told you that already. You changed that. [KÜR-MANN *stands there at a loss.*] Why don't you work? She's right: is your marriage the only thing you can think of?

KÜRMANN. Be quiet.

RECORDER. Is that your only problem? [KÜRMANN *stands in silence.*] Do you want to go back again?

KÜRMANN. What for?

RECORDER. As you like.

FRAU HUBALEK *comes in with mail.*

KÜRMANN. Thank you, Frau Hubalek, thank you.

FRAU HUBALEK *goes out.*

RECORDER. Your paperback is out.

KÜRMANN. At last.

RECORDER. How do you like it?

KÜRMANN *leafs through the book, then stops.*

KÜRMANN. What else has happened?

ANTOINETTE *comes in wearing her coat.*

ANTOINETTE. I'm going now, Hannes.

RECORDER. Evidently you're still married.

ANTOINETTE. I'm going now, Hannes.

KÜRMANN. To town.

ANTOINETTE. To town.

KÜRMANN. You'll be spending the afternoon in the library.

ANTOINETTE. I'll be spending the afternoon in the library.

KÜRMANN. You'll be back in the evening.

ANTOINETTE. I don't know about that yet. [*She leaves.*]

KÜRMANN. She doesn't know about that yet! [*He throws the paper-back in the corner.*]

RECORDER. Don't you like the make-up of the book? [KÜRMANN *drops into the easy chair.*] That was 1964. [*He reads from the dossier.*] "Khrushchev is dismissed. / The assassination of President Kennedy in Dallas, Texas, remains unsolved. / The Bundeswehr attains the goal set by NATO of twelve divisions——"

KÜRMANN. What happened a year later?

RECORDER. 1965. [*He reads from the dossier.*] "Launching of the Soviet spacecraft Voskhod II. Leonov leaves the spaceship through an air lock and is the first man to float in space. He remains there for ten minutes. Manual landing after seventeen orbits of the earth."

KÜRMANN. Frau Hubalek!

RECORDER. Why are you shouting?

KÜRMANN. Why hasn't breakfast been cleared away? Frau Hubalek! Why doesn't she clear away? Frau Hubalek!

*A young Italian girl comes in.*

PINA. *Professore desidera?*

RECORDER. Frau Hubalek is dead.

KÜRMANN. *La tavola. Prego. Per favore.*

RECORDER. Her name is Pina and she comes from Calabria.

KÜRMANN. *Come sta, Pina?*

PINA. *Meglio, signore, molto meglio. Grazie.*

KÜRMANN. *Brutto tempo in questo paese.*

PINA. Eh.

KÜRMANN. Eh.

*PINA takes the breakfast things and goes out.*

RECORDER. Your Italian is making progress.

KÜRMANN. What else?

RECORDER. You're getting older. [*He looks in his dossier.*] You're now forty-eight, Herr Kürmann. In two years you will be fifty. [*He looks at Kürmann.*] What are you thinking about? [KÜRMANN *sits in silence.*] Those dreams in which all your teeth fall out and you feel them in your mouth like loose pebbles are nothing new, but you've been having them more often recently——

KÜRMANN. What else?

RECORDER. You're not gaga yet.

KÜRMANN. Thanks.

RECORDER. Word of honor! Even if your son, Thomas, holds a different opinion. [THOMAS *enters. He has a Beatle haircut.*] That's the way people wear their hair nowadays.

KÜRMANN. I don't need his opinion.

THOMAS. That's just it. That's why it's impossible to talk to him. I'm sick and tired of hearing, when I was your age! Maybe things were the way he says, but they aren't any more. He's always going on about his biography. [*He sits on the desk.*] I live like this, and that's all there is to it.

KÜRMANN. So I see.

THOMAS. So what? [*He dangles his jacket.*] He simply isn't with it any more. What's the use of experience? No one who is with it believes in Marxism-Leninism any more. For example. Except the Chinese, who've just got there——

RECORDER. Thomas is now twenty-three.

THOMAS. What did you want to say to me?

KÜRMANN. Nothing.

THOMAS. Okay.

KÜRMANN. You're young, Thomas, but for the moment that's about all you are. You and your hair! What do you know about yourself? That you do what you like. Have you ever yet admitted a mistake and gone on living with it?

RECORDER. Herr Kürmann, that isn't what you wanted to say.

KÜRMANN. Have you ever yet admitted a mistake and gone on living with it? It's perfectly true. What have you ever gone through, you mushroomheads? What, I ask you? [*He shouts.*] Well, what?

THOMAS. Now you're acting like an old man, Dad.

KÜRMANN *says nothing.*

RECORDER. Why did you say that again?

THOMAS *has gone.*

KÜRMANN. What else happened?

ANTOINETTE *comes in wearing her coat.*

ANTOINETTE. I'm going now, Hannes.

RECORDER. One moment. [*He leafs through the dossier.*] Of course all sorts of things have happened. You haven't been standing around in that dressing gown year in, year out. For example, you have been to Russia in the meantime.

KÜRMANN. How was it?

RECORDER. You've said nothing about it. Up to now. You were there almost half a year; it wasn't possible to meet Krolevsky. You realize, Herr Kürmann, that certain people imagine they can deduce from your silence that you were disappointed by Russia.

ANTOINETTE. So he was.

KÜRMANN. How do you know?

ANTOINETTE. Egon was in Russia too.

KÜRMANN. Egon!

ANTOINETTE. He gave an account of his visit.

KÜRMANN. Egon is a reactionary.

ANTOINETTE. Whereas you keep quiet because you are a progressive. [*She has no time to continue.*] Well, I'm going now.

KÜRMANN. Why don't we get a divorce?

ANTOINETTE. I'll be back in the evening.

KÜRMANN. I asked you a question.

ANTOINETTE. I beg your pardon?

KÜRMANN. Why don't we get a divorce?

*Pause.*

RECORDER. She expects an explanation. In the first version you gave the following explanation that morning. [*He reads from the dossier.*] "We're wasting our time, Antoinette. I love you, but we're wasting our time."

KÜRMANN. Wasting our time.

RECORDER. "We only live once."

KÜRMANN. Did I say that?

RECORDER. Trite but heartfelt. [*He reads from the dossier.*] "Once, years ago, you remember, you said: if anything changes between us, I'll tell you."

ANTOINETTE. Yes.

RECORDER. "But nothing will change; Egon is a Catholic."

ANTOINETTE. What do you mean by that?

RECORDER. "He can't get a divorce."

ANTOINETTE. No.

RECORDER. "That sanctifies our marriage too."

KÜRMANN. So that's how it is.

RECORDER. "I know you don't like to be talked to in this tone, but nevertheless I'm in favor of our getting divorced."

KÜRMANN. Without delay.

RECORDER. "We can." [ANTOINETTE *sits down*.] Do you want to change this conversation?

KÜRMANN. I hoped it wouldn't come to that. I behaved like a man of experience. I didn't open any letters and so on. I hoped——

RECORDER. ——that Egon would disappear.

KÜRMANN. Yes.

RECORDER. But he didn't.

KÜRMANN. No.

RECORDER. So you want a divorce again?

KÜRMANN. Without delay.

*Pause.* ANTOINETTE *takes a cigarette.*

ANTOINETTE. Have you talked to a lawyer?

KÜRMANN. No.

ANTOINETTE. I've talked to a lawyer. He told me it would be easier if we both had the same lawyer. He told me, if the suit was contested, it would take at least a year. . . . [*She lights her cigarette and smokes.*]

KÜRMANN. What happens in a year?

RECORDER. It's 1966.

KÜRMANN. What happens then? [A *baby is heard yelling*.] A baby?

RECORDER. Yes.

KÜRMANN. By him?

RECORDER. No.

KÜRMANN. By me?

RECORDER. No.

KÜRMANN. Who by?

RECORDER. The Calabrian girl has a baby. [*The baby stops yelling*.] What else has happened? [*He looks in the dossier*.] The Kürmann reflex, a concept which at one time had gained a number of adherents, has been proved by subsequent research untenable.

*The baby cries again.*

ANTOINETTE. I'm going now, Hannes. [*She stubs out her cigarette*.] Either we go to a lawyer and get a divorce, or we never discuss the matter again. There's nothing we haven't already said to each other. [*She rises.*] I'll be spending the afternoon in the library.

KÜRMANN. You'll be spending the afternoon in the library.

ANTOINETTE. I'll be back in the evening.

KÜRMANN. You'll be back in the evening.

ANTOINETTE. Otherwise I'll ring. [*She leaves.*]

RECORDER. At this point, Herr Kürmann, you said, if you could begin all over again, you knew exactly what you would do differently. [KÜRMANN *stands motionless.*] Do you want to begin all over again? [KÜRMANN *stands motionless.*] You love her. [KÜRMANN *goes to the bookcase and takes a revolver from behind the books, standing so that the* RECORDER *cannot see what he is doing. He releases the safety catch as quietly as possible.*] You reached that point once before. You were going to shoot yourself because you thought you couldn't live without her—then you came to the conclusion that that was mawkishly sentimental. [*He looks it up in the dossier.*] September 1966. [*The sound of the cracked piano from next door again, the same bars of music broken off and repeated, while the* RECORDER *lights a cigarette; then silence.*] We too, I must frankly admit, expected something different from a man who had the opportunity of starting over again—something bolder.

KÜRMANN. Yes.

RECORDER. Nothing grandiose, perhaps, but something different, something you hadn't already lived through once before. At least something different. [*He smokes. Neon lamp off.*] For example, why didn't you emigrate?

[*Projection:* KÜRMANN *in a sola topee.*]

Kürmann in the Philippines studying the behavior of birds that don't exist at our latitude. The life of a scientist, hard but meaningful. . . .

KÜRMANN. Yes.

RECORDER. Ask this Kürmann what he thinks of Hornacher. At first he won't remember; then he'll laugh. Or ask him about a certain Egon.

[*Projection:* KÜRMANN *with ladies.*]

Or. Kürmann as a *bon viveur*.

Kürmann. Skip that.

Recorder. I don't know whether you were thinking of something like that when you said, if you could begin all over again, and so on.

Kürmann. What do you take me for?

Recorder. At least it would have been different. . . .

[*Projection:* Kürmann *in an academic gown.*]

If you didn't emigrate—*ubi bene, ibi patria*—then you would only have needed patience and a little tactical skill, the sense to keep your mouth shut when to speak would have given offense, and we'd have had Kürmann as rector. Now you would be making the decisions where Hornacher is making them. That wouldn't change the world, but it would change the University a bit, one of many.

[*Projection:* Kürmann *in a brawl.*]

Why didn't you go out into the streets?

[*Projection:* Kürmann *with Katrin and children.*]

Since you were able to choose again, why didn't you try, for example, to prevent Katrin's suicide? Perhaps it would have been enough for her to have a garden full of children, children playing shuttlecock.

Kürmann. Be quiet.

Recorder. Kürmann as a daddy on Sunday. [*The cracked piano from next door again playing the same bars of music, repeated, while the projections disappear. Silence.*] Instead we have the same flat. The same trouble with Antoinette. Only without a slap in the face. You've changed that. Also, you've joined the Party, but that hasn't turned you into a different person. What else? You're more or less sticking to a diet. Those are the only changes you've made—this whole performance just for that!

Kürmann. I love her.

Antoinette *comes in wearing a coat.*

Antoinette. I'm going now, Hannes. [Kürmann *looks at the revolver in his hand.*] I'm going now, Hannes.

Kürmann. I heard you.

Antoinette. Don't forget, we have guests tonight. The Schneiders are coming. And Henrik. And a few other people——

KÜRMANN. You'll be spending the afternoon at the library.

ANTOINETTE. Didn't you hear what I said?

KÜRMANN. And a few others.

ANTOINETTE. I'll be spending the afternoon at the library.

KÜRMANN *turns around, and because he happens to have the revolver in his hand, and because he is sick of talking, he aims at* ANTOINETTE *and fires the first shot.* ANTOINETTE *does not back away or collapse.*

ANTOINETTE. Hannes——

*Second shot.*

KÜRMANN. She thinks I'm dreaming this.

*Third shot.*

ANTOINETTE. I'm going now, Hannes.

KÜRMANN. To town.

ANTOINETTE. To town. [*Fourth shot.*] I'll be back in the evening.

*Fifth shot.* ANTOINETTE *collapses.*

RECORDER. Yes, Herr Kürmann, now you have fired.

KÜRMANN. Me?

*Working light. The whole stage is visible. A gray wall is lowered, hiding the room. Two* STAGEHANDS *place a prison cot in front of it and leave.*

*Acting light.* KÜRMANN *appears in convict clothes.*

RECORDER. You may sit down. [KÜRMANN *sits down. The* RECORDER *takes the dossier and sits down beside* KÜRMANN.] On the morning of 4/29/1966, without any significant dispute having taken place, you fired five shots at your wife, Antoinette Kürmann, nee Stein, Ph.D. The fifth shot, in the head, proved fatal. . . . While held in custody, you stated that you had intended to commit suicide with the sixth bullet, which was still in the magazine. Instead, according to the dossier, you informed the police and made a full confession. . . . And so on. [*He turns the pages.*] On being asked whether you felt remorse, you replied that you were surprised, you didn't think you had it in you. [KÜRMANN *says nothing.*] According to the psychiatrist's report, there is no evidence of insanity. . . . And so on. [*He turns the pages.*] Financial circumstances.

[*He turns the pages.*] Past history of the accused. [*He turns the pages.*] Past history of the victim. [*He turns the pages.*] At one point you declared, in response to the question of why you had fired upon your totally unsuspecting wife, I quote: "I suddenly knew what was coming." At another point, I quote: "My wife said she was going to spend the afternoon at the library, or she was on the point of saying it, and as I knew this sentence already and was sick of it, I fired at this sentence, so to speak, in order not to hear it again." [KÜRMANN *says nothing.*] The sentence was life imprisonment. You waived your right to a final speech before sentence was passed. . . . Don't you want to appeal?

KÜRMANN. No.

RECORDER. May I now ask you a question? [*Pause.*] In the face of this biography, do you think—or rather, do you believe—do you feel, now that you're living in this cell, a—how shall I put it—an inclination, yes, an inclination, a need, a readiness with which you were previously unfamiliar and that has only arisen out of the consciousness of guilt, a . . . readiness . . .

KÜRMANN. To do what?

RECORDER. To begin with, you will stay in this cell; later you will work on the land or perhaps in the carpenters' shop; later perhaps in the office, clerical work and that kind of thing. . . . You are now forty-nine, Herr Kürmann. A remission of sentence, which everyone knows is possible as a reward for good behavior, cannot be expected for twelve years. By then you will be sixty-one, assuming you live that long. . . . You understand my question?

KÜRMANN. You mean, in order to bear this prospect I must look around for a meaning for what happened.

RECORDER. I'm asking.

KÜRMANN. And this meaning would lie in my believing that this and this alone was bound to happen. Something that can never be proved but only believed. This and this alone. Destiny. Providence.

RECORDER. You can put it like that.

KÜRMANN. I know how it happened.

RECORDER. By chance?

KÜRMANN. It wasn't inevitable.

*Pause.*

RECORDER. Herr Kürmann, you have the choice.

KÜRMANN. To believe or not to believe.

RECORDER. Yes.

> KÜRMANN *rises, walks through the cell, stands still.*

KÜRMANN. And her? What about her? . . . Whether I believe or
not, what difference does that make to her? It's her life—not my
life. . . . What good will it do the one who is dead if I, her
murderer, paper my cell with destiny? I have destroyed a life—her
life. How does choice come into it? She is dead—dead—and I
choose to believe or not to believe. [*He laughs.*] Remorse! What
you call remorse——

RECORDER. What do you mean?

KÜRMANN. Antoinette could live—that didn't have to happen. Live
—that means eat, laugh, dream of her gallery that never comes
into existence, have a child by someone, lie, sleep, wear a new
dress—live. . . .

> *The* RECORDER *rises.*

RECORDER. Then let us go back again. [*Neon lamp on. He goes to his
lectern, where he tears the last few pages out of the dossier and
throws them into the wastepaper basket.*] Go ahead. [*Neon lamp
off.*]

*The gray wall disappears upward. Acting light in the room. A small
party in jovial mood toward morning; ladies and gentlemen sitting on
the floor;* ANTOINETTE *is sitting at the spinet playing, but the guests
are not listening, apart from a fair-haired man standing by the bookcase; the rest are drinking or flirting or laughing.* ANTOINETTE *stops
playing.*

ANTOINETTE. I haven't played for years.

> *Laughter.*

HENRIK. Antoinette is a genius. Where's Kürmann? Someone ought
to tell him that Antoinette is a genius. Kürmann!

SOMEONE. Don't yell.

HENRIK. Someone ought to tell him.

> *Pause.*

FIRST LADY. Heavens, it's time we were off.

SOMEONE. What was that about garden dwarfs?

FIRST LADY. Herr Kürmann has to work tomorrow.

ANTOINETTE. Shall I make some gruel? [*No one moves.*] I'll make some gruel.

*A lady squeaks.*

HENRIK. What are you doing with my wife?

SECOND LADY. You're hurting me.

SCHNEIDER. Who?

SECOND LADY. You.

SCHNEIDER. That's not me.

*Laughter.*

HENRIK. Muggy!

SECOND LADY. Don't keep yelling all the time.

HENRIK. Why aren't you a genius?

SECOND LADY. Henrik, you're starting to get silly.

HENRIK. Antoinette is a genius. How can a man simply disappear when it turns out that his wife is a genius? I'm coming increasingly to the opinion that Antoinette is a genius who hasn't played for years.

SECOND LADY. Henrik is tight.

ANTOINETTE. Shall I make some gruel?

SCHNEIDER. I've been hearing that question for the last hour. . . .

*Silence.*

SOMEONE. An angel is passing through the room!

KÜRMANN *in the foreground, dressed as a convict, has been watching. Now he passes through the room and disappears, unnoticed by anyone.*

HENRIK. Schneider!

SCHNEIDER. Don't yell.

HENRIK. Do you want some gruel?

ANTOINETTE. Who wants some gruel?

SOMEONE. What was that about garden dwarfs?

SCHNEIDER. Who wants some gruel?

SOMEONE. Garden dwarfs.

SEVERAL. Gruel!

SEVERAL. Garden dwarfs!

*Glasses clink.*

HENRIK. That's the result.

SCHNEIDER. What of?

HENRIK. No one's listening to me. [FIRST LADY *has risen.*] Frau Stahel wants to leave.

FIRST LADY. It's time.

HENRIK. Frau Stahel has three children.

ANTOINETTE *goes to the fair-haired man.*

HENRIK. Antoinette!

SCHNEIDER. Keep quiet.

HENRIK. No whispering here.

*The fair-haired man sits down at the spinet.*

HENRIK. Stahel!

SOMEONE. What's happened to the gruel?

HENRIK. Your wife wants to leave, your wife has three children—— [STAHEL *plays the spinet; he plays better than* ANTOINETTE, *and gradually people actually begin to listen.* KÜRMANN *appears in a dressing gown and is not noticed at first.*] Kürmann has been resurrected. . . . Your resurrection doesn't impress anybody, Kürmann, but you've got a magnificent wife, Kürmann, if you want to know. You don't deserve a wife like that.

KÜRMANN *goes up to* ANTOINETTE.

KÜRMANN. I'll make some gruel. [*Applause that interrupts the piano-playing.*] But it will take a little while. [*He goes out.*]

HENRIK. You don't deserve a husband like that, Antoinette, if you want to know. You don't deserve each other.

SECOND LADY. Let Egon go on playing.

HENRIK. Muggy!

SECOND LADY. What is it?

HENRIK. Why can't you listen when I need you as a witness? Have I ever made gruel?

SECOND LADY. No.

STAHEL *goes on playing.* KÜRMANN *appears beside the* RECORDER.

RECORDER. I thought you were going to make some gruel. What's the matter? Don't you feel well? Your friends are waiting for the gruel.

KÜRMANN. What happens in a year?

RECORDER. Do you want to know?

KÜRMANN. What happens in a year?

*A white wall is lowered, hiding the room.* KÜRMANN *stands in front of it. A* NURSE *in white enters with a wheel chair.*

NURSE. You shouldn't have gotten up, Herr Kürmann, three weeks after the operation. [*She leads* KÜRMANN *to the wheel chair.*] You must be patient, Herr Kürmann. [*She covers him with a rug.*] Are you feeling any pain? [*The* NURSE *leaves.*]

RECORDER. You're going to have an injection in a minute.

*The piano-playing stops.*

KÜRMANN. What has happened?

RECORDER. 1967. [*He reads from the dossier.*] "Military dictatorship in Greece——"

KÜRMANN *interrupts him.*

KÜRMANN. How long have I been in this hospital?

RECORDER. Since January.

KÜRMANN. It's June now.

RECORDER. That's right.

KÜRMANN. It's not my liver.

RECORDER. No.

KÜRMANN. What is it then?

RECORDER. You looked after your liver.

KÜRMANN. No one tells me what it is.

RECORDER. The chief physician says it's gastritis.

KÜRMANN. First of all they said they didn't know.

RECORDER. An unusually protracted attack of gastritis.

*The* NURSE *brings a chair and goes again.*

KÜRMANN. Why doesn't anyone tell me?

*A gentleman with a black monocle appears from the left.*

RECORDER. Do you want any visitors?

KÜRMANN. No.

RECORDER. That was Snottler. You remember: the snowball fight. But he made his way in the world, as you can see, even without a left eye. Commercial attaché. He wants to tell you about South Africa, a man with lots of stories to tell. He wants to cheer you up—everyone is down on their·luck at times. [A *lady appears.*] Frau Stahel.

KÜRMANN. What does she want?

RECORDER. Nothing.

KÜRMANN. Then why has she come?

RECORDER. She feels the need. Egon is already in Brazil; she will be joining him at Christmas with the children. She simply feels the need. [A *man with a little beard enters.*] Who are you? [*The man looks around the room.*] He wants to talk to you alone. [A *lady and gentleman enter.*] The Schneiders. [KÜRMANN *closes his eyes.*] Herr Kürmann is in pain just at the moment. [A *young woman enters.*] That was Marlis.

KÜRMANN. Who?

RECORDER. Marlis was important to you at a time when you doubted whether you were still a man at all. People are grateful for having been important. Marlis too only wants to cheer you up. She heard yesterday quite by chance that you had been in the hospital for months.

KÜRMANN. Marlis?

RECORDER. Marlis is stupid, but she knows it. Perhaps she will start talking about metastasis, merely because she muddles up foreign words. [A *gentleman in a camel's-hair coat enters.*] Herr Witzig, known as Henrik, advertising consultant. [*The man with the little beard starts to go.*] Don't go!

KÜRMANN. Krolevsky?

RECORDER. He has recognized you. [KROLEVSKY *sits down; the other visitors leave.*] Vladimir Krolevsky, born in Riga, Latvia, the son of a rabbi; escaped an SS roundup because he was erroneously taken for dead; later a partisan on Lake Ladoga, where he was wounded; a student of mathematics at Leningrad; forced labor for a time under Stalin, later rehabilitated; since 1958 an agent in the West; 1960 dismissed from his teaching post and extradited; returned to Moscow; condemned as a revisionist; escaped through

Finland. For two years ex-Professor Krolevsky, alias Carlo Ferrari, a member of the Italian Communist party, has been working in Turin. But he doesn't want to talk about that until you're well.

KÜRMANN. What does he think about the war in Israel?

RECORDER. He's for Nasser.

KÜRMANN. Against Israel? [KROLEVSKY *makes a gesture.*] What does he say?

RECORDER. He says, of course—naturally.

KÜRMANN. Why?

RECORDER. Comrade Krolevsky doesn't want to talk about that until you're well, Herr Kürmann.

*The* NURSE *comes in with flowers.*

NURSE. Just look, Herr Kürmann, just look. Flowers from your son in America. [*She removes the tissue paper.*] Lovely roses!

KÜRMANN. Sister Agnes——

NURSE. A loving son.

KÜRMANN. Can I speak to the chief physician?

*The* NURSE *arranges the roses.*

NURSE. At once, Herr Kürmann, at once.

RECORDER. Why don't you give him an injection?

NURSE. At once, Herr Kürmann, at once.

*The* DOCTOR *enters in a white coat, accompanied by a young* ASSISTANT. KROLEVSKY *leaves.*

DOCTOR. Well, Herr Kürmann, how are we? How did we sleep last night? [*To the* NURSE.] Did Herr Kürmann manage to eat anything?

NURSE. Some tea.

*The* DOCTOR *takes the report from the* NURSE *and studies it.*

DOCTOR. You see, Herr Kürmann, you're gradually feeling better. [*He gives the report to his* ASSISTANT.] Herr Kürmann wants to start going for walks already! [*He takes* KÜRMANN *by the shoulder.*] Feeling tired? That comes from the radiation; it doesn't mean anything. We shall give you a bit more radiation, nonetheless. [*He makes introductions.*] My new assistant—Doctor Fink.

ASSISTANT. Funk.

DOCTOR. He will look after you while I'm on vacation. I believe Dr. Fink also plays chess. [*He is about to shake hands.*] We shall see each other again in three weeks, Herr Kürmann——

KÜRMANN. Professor——

DOCTOR. We must be patient.

KÜRMANN. ——can I speak to you? [ASSISTANT *and* NURSE *leave.*] Do you know what it is yet?

DOCTOR. You worry too much.

KÜRMANN. You can speak frankly.

DOCTOR. Gastritis. [*He takes off his glasses and polishes them.*] An unusually protracted attack of gastritis. . . . [*He holds his glasses up to the light to see if they are clean.*] I know what you're thinking; that's the first thing people think of when they hear the word radiation. [*He puts his glasses on again.*] Don't worry. As I said, I shall be back in three weeks. [KÜRMANN *says nothing.*] You'll like Dr. Fink.

KÜRMANN. Funk.

DOCTOR. A conscientious man. [*He takes his glasses off again and holds them up to the light.*] Actually I was intending to go to Greece, but after what's just been happening . . . [*He puts his glasses on again.*] Would you go to Greece at the present time? [KÜRMANN *says nothing.*] Herr Kürmann.

KÜRMANN. Yes.

DOCTOR. We must be patient.

KÜRMANN. Did you operate for gastritis?

DOCTOR. No.

KÜRMANN. Why was I operated on?

DOCTOR. You weren't operated on, Herr Kürmann.

KÜRMANN. Then why was I told——

DOCTOR. Who told you?

KÜRMANN. Sister Agnes.

*The* DOCTOR *sits down.*

DOCTOR. I can speak frankly to you——

KÜRMANN. It won't go any further.

DOCTOR. Naturally we thought of that too—I won't hide that—otherwise we shouldn't have considered operating.

KÜRMANN. Why nuclear radiation?

DOCTOR. You must realize that nuclear radiation is a precaution. As long as you are here, I mean until we are certain, I mean quite certain, that this gastritis won't come back—you've probably had this gastritis before, pains in the stomach, but you thought it was your liver. . . . But we want to do everything possible, Herr Kürmann, to make sure it doesn't become chronic. [*Pause.*] What beautiful flowers you've got today!

KÜRMANN. From my son.

DOCTOR. You've got a son?

KÜRMANN. In America.

DOCTOR. I didn't know that.

KÜRMANN. He won a scholarship.

DOCTOR. What is he studying?

KÜRMANN. Film technique.

DOCTOR. Aha.

KÜRMANN. He's gifted.

*Pause.*

DOCTOR. As I was saying, Herr Kürmann, we must do everything possible to make sure it doesn't become chronic. Radiation is unpleasant, we know that. How old are you now? Of course, there's a certain danger at our age; statistics prove that. All the same, it would be irresponsible not to do everything possible. . . .[*The* DOCTOR *rises.*]

KÜRMANN. Thank you.

DOCTOR. What are you reading? [*He picks up a book.*] *Italian Without Tears.* [*He turns the pages.*] You would like to know when you can start traveling again; I can understand that. [*He puts the book down again.*] Chianciano is still beautiful in autumn—in fact even more beautiful. . . .

KÜRMANN. I'm simply scared.

DOCTOR. Of the radiation?

KÜRMANN. Of dying by inches. [*Knock at the door.*] Does my wife know?

*Knock at the door.*

DOCTOR. To tell you the truth, we don't know what it is.

ANTOINETTE *enters wearing a coat. The* DOCTOR *goes to meet her and shakes hands with her. They stand to one side whispering.*

KÜRMANN. What are you whispering about? [*The* DOCTOR *leaves.*] You always said I could choose.

RECORDER. Yes.

KÜRMANN. What can I choose?

RECORDER. How you react to the fact that you're done for.

ANTOINETTE *comes closer.*

ANTOINETTE. I got you the books. [*She takes books out of a bag.*] Are you in pain?

KÜRMANN. They're going to give me an injection.

ANTOINETTE *sits down.*

ANTOINETTE. Have you had visitors?

KÜRMANN. Yes, I think so.

ANTOINETTE. Who was here?

KÜRMANN. Marlis.

ANTOINETTE. Who is Marlis?

KÜRMANN. Marlis.

ANTOINETTE. Marlis?

KÜRMANN. I don't remember. . . .

The NURSE *comes with the hypodermic syringe.*

NURSE. Herr Kürmann.

KÜRMANN. Don't go away!

NURSE. In a minute you'll feel better. [*She gives him the injection.*] We're going to do the radiation at eleven. [*She dabs the needle mark.*] In a minute Herr Kürmann will feel better. [*The* NURSE *leaves.*]

KÜRMANN. I wanted to go out into the garden today. [ANTOINETTE *picks up the book.*] I've been talking to him. . . . We spoke very frankly. [ANTOINETTE *starts in dismay.*] They don't know what it is. . . . He says Chianciano can also be beautiful in autumn. If we go with the car, everything is within reach; I looked it up on the map. One hundred ninety miles to Rome, eighty miles to Siena. All just a stone's throw.

ANTOINETTE. Yes, Hannes, yes.

KÜRMANN. Do you know Siena?

ANTOINETTE. Yes, Hannes, yes.

KÜRMANN. I don't.

> ANTOINETTE *opens the textbook.*

ANTOINETTE. Where did we get to?

KÜRMANN. *Decima Lezione.*

ANTOINETTE. What would the gentleman like?

KÜRMANN. *Che cosa desidera il Signore?*

ANTOINETTE. *Il Signore desidera.*

KÜRMANN. *Vorrei una cravatta.*

ANTOINETTE. Where is the mirror?

KÜRMANN. *Dove c'è un specchio?*

ANTOINETTE. *Dove si trova——*

KÜRMANN. *Dove si trova uno specchio?*

ANTOINETTE. The mirror.

KÜRMANN. *Dove si trova il specchio?*

ANTOINETTE. *Lo specchio.*

KÜRMANN. *Lo specchio, lo studio, lo spazio.*

ANTOINETTE. Plural.

KÜRMANN. *Gli specchi.*

ANTOINETTE. Lesson Eleven. [KÜRMANN *remains silent.*] What's the matter, Hannes?

KÜRMANN. There was something I wanted to write to you. When you're here, they always give me an injection; then I can't remember what it was.

> *Neon lamp on.*

RECORDER. I made a note of it. [*He reads from a slip of paper.*] "We diminished one another. Why did we always diminish one another? I you, you me. Why was everything that was possible for us so diminished? We only know each other diminished." [*He puts away the slip of paper.*] That was all that occurred to you when you were not under the influence of morphia.

> *Neon lamp off.*

ANTOINETTE. Lesson Eleven.

KÜRMANN. *Undicesima Lezione.* [*The young* ASSISTANT *enters.*] They want to irradiate me again.

ANTOINETTE *rises.*

ANTOINETTE. I'll come back in the afternoon. [*The young* ASSISTANT *wheels* KÜRMANN *out.* ANTOINETTE *is now alone.*] He knows!

RECORDER. Sometimes, not all the time. . . . [*Long pause.* ANTOINETTE *stands motionless.*] Yes. . . . It may go on for months, and you come every day—twice a day now. You can't save him either, Frau Kürmann; you know that. . . . In ten years, perhaps—who knows?—or even in one year there will be some cure, but now it is still destiny. . . . [ANTOINETTE *is about to leave.*] Frau Kürmann.

ANTOINETTE. Yes?

RECORDER. Do you regret the seven years with him? [ANTOINETTE *stares at the* RECORDER.] If I told you that you too have the choice, you too can start all over again, would you know what you would do differently in your life?

ANTOINETTE. Yes.

RECORDER. Yes?

ANTOINETTE. Yes.

RECORDER. Then go ahead. . . . [*The* RECORDER *leads* ANTOINETTE *out.*] You too can choose all over again.

*Working light. The room is in position again.*

*Acting light.* ANTOINETTE *enters in evening dress and sits down in the easy chair and waits. She is wearing her horn-rimmed spectacles. As at the beginning of the play, there are voices and laughter from outside. Soon afterward* KÜRMANN *enters, whistling to himself until he sees the young lady.*

ANTOINETTE. "I'm going soon too."

*Silence; he stands there at a loss, then begins to clear away bottles and glasses and ash trays; then he is once more at a loss.*

KÜRMANN. "Don't you feel well?"

ANTOINETTE. "On the contrary." [*She takes a cigarette.*] "Just one more cigarette." [*She waits in vain for a light.*] "If I'm not in the way." [*She lights her cigarette and smokes.*] "I enjoyed it very

much. Some of them were very nice, I thought, very stimulating. . . ." [*Silence.*] "Have you anything left to drink?"

KÜRMANN *goes and pours a glass of whisky.*

KÜRMANN. "Ice?" [*He hands her the whisky.*]

ANTOINETTE. "What about you?"

KÜRMAN. "I have to work tomorrow."

ANTOINETTE. "What do you do?"

A *clock strikes two.*

KÜRMANN. "It's two o'clock."

ANTOINETTE. "Are you expecting someone?"

KÜRMANN. "On the contrary."

ANTOINETTE. "You're tired."

KÜRMANN. "I'm ready to drop."

ANTOINETTE. "Why don't you sit down?" [KÜRMANN *remains standing and says nothing.*] "I can't drink any quicker." [*Pause.*] "I
really only wanted to hear your old musical clock again. Musical
clocks fascinate me. The way the figures always go through the
same movements as soon as the music starts. It always plays the
same waltz, and yet you can't wait to see what happens each
time." [*She slowly empties her glass.*] "Don't you feel the same?"

KÜRMANN *goes to the musical clock and winds it up; there is a gay
tinkling; he winds until the waltz is at an end.*

KÜRMANN. "Is there anything else I can do for you?"

ANTOINETTE *stubs out her cigarette.*

ANTOINETTE. "I'm going now."

KÜRMANN. "Have you a car?"

ANTOINETTE. Yes. [*She stands up and takes the jacket of her evening
dress.*] "Why are you looking at me like that?" [*She puts on her
jacket.*] "Why are you looking at me like that?" [ANTOINETTE
*picks up her handbag;* KÜRMANN *stands looking at her, as though
he does not believe she intends to go.*] "I have to work tomorrow
as well."

KÜRMANN *goes with her to the elevator; the room remains empty for
a while; then* KÜRMANN *comes back.*

KÜRMANN. What now?

RECORDER. Now she has gone.

KÜRMANN. What now?

RECORDER. And now you're free.

KÜRMANN. Free. . . .

*Neon light on. The* RECORDER *opens the dossier.*

RECORDER. "May 26, 1960. I had guests. It got late. When the guests had finally left, she was just sitting there. What can you do with an unknown woman who doesn't leave, who just sits there without speaking at two in the morning? It need not have happened." [*He turns the page.*] You've got a meeting tomorrow at eleven. . . . [*He puts the dossier down on the desk open and steps back. Neon light off.*] Go ahead. [KÜRMANN *stands motionless.*] You're free— for another seven years. . . .

*Curtain.*